Published by G.W. Kent, Inc.
3667 Morgan Rd.
Ann Arbor, MI 48108 U.S.A.

1st printing 1993

ISBN 0-9619072-0-7

Printed in U.S.A.

The American Wine Society Presents

GROWING WINE GRAPES

Table of Contents

About The Authors

JOHN R. McGREW

After receiving a PhD. in plant pathology he joined the fruit laboratory at the USDA Agricultural Research Service. By the time of his retirement Dr. McGrew was in charge of the grape breeding projects. Using a collection of native species as sources of black rot resistance, several breeding lines carrying resistance to both black rot and powdery mildew were distributed to experiment stations for further refinement. He has been growing wine grapes at home for 40 years. He currently maintains a half-acre vineyard and has won many awards for his homemade wines.

JUERGEN LOENHOLDT

Mr. Loenholdt has grown wine grapes for several decades. He was director of Viticultural Research for the Taylor Wine Company.

THOMAS J. ZABADAL

Dr. Zabadal received his PhD. from Cornell University. He is currently the coordinator of Michigan State University's Southwest Michigan Research and Extension Center.

ARTHUR C. HUNT

Mr. Hunt is a vineyard and winery management consultant. He also owns "Hunt Country Vineyards" which has won many awards for its Germanic style Late Harvest wines.

HERMAN O. AMBERG

Mr. Amberg graduated from the Horticultural College in Geisenheim, Germany. For the past 40 years he has done research on grape rootsocks, winter cold tolerance and training systems. Mr. Amberg now owns "Grafted Grapevine Nursery" and "Amberg Wine Cellars".

CHAPTER ONE

GUIDE TO WINE GRAPE GROWING

By John R. McGREW, Ph.D.

GRAPE QUALITY IS THE MAJOR FACTOR FOR DETERMINING WINE QUALITY

THE WINEMAKER can use such techniques as cool fermentation, oak-aging or carbonic maceration to enhance certain table wines, but the quality of the finished wine is still dependent on the quality of the grapes. The winemaker who accepts the responsibilities of also growing the grapes can realize the highest potential for his wines. As a grower, he can choose the best adapted varieties, grow them properly, control the size of the crop for proper balance, and harvest at the optimum stage.

This book is for the home grape grower-winemaker who would like to produce the best possible wines. Because $1/4$ acre (at 5 tons per acre) will equal the maximum legal production of 200 gallons of wine per year, some of the suggestions are geared to a modest home-vineyard and may be impractical for larger vineyards. The equipment and practices required for large vineyard operations do reduce labor input, but many of these are at the expense of fruit quality.

ROLE OF THE VINEYARDIST

The Growing Of Grapes Is Work.

It requires time and effort to prune and repair trellises during the dormant season.

It requires nearly constant attention during the growing season.

It requires a long range dedication when the first rewards are not realized until three years after planting.

It also requires a calm and forgiving personality to shrug off the disaster of crop loss from hail, frost, herbicide drift or other acts-of-nature.

1

If the vineyard is located so far away from your residence that a special effort must be made to see how it is growing, you risk the damages that result from failure to do the little timely chores. Skip one weekend, or take a two week vacation, and you risk an explosive buildup of destructive insects or diseases.

The vineyardist must be able to recognize and defend against the many threats to the crop. Such skills are acquired by training and experience.

Size Of The Vineyard

It requires little more effort to grow 10 vines than one, but at about 50 vines, one begins to long for additional equipment to help with the tasks. At 100 vines, additional equipment becomes the difference between a hobby and a chore. By 250 vines (a half acre), power equipment (tractor with mower, power sprayer, etc.) becomes a necessity. It is better to start small and do a conscientious job than to plant so many vines that the vineyard does not receive the necessary care.

Vineyard Site

The most important single factor that determines the eventual success of a vineyard is the site. The "ideal" site is one that fulfills the requirements of full sunlight, soil fertility and drainage, available moisture, sufficient slope and proper configuration for frost protection and is also an open area where there is usually a breeze during the growing season.

Most of us look over the property we already own and pick the area that best matches these conditions. This generally involves some compromises which may not prevent the growing of wine grapes, but may restrict the varieties that will be successful.

The site is probably the basic source of the conflict between the so-called "hybridists" and "viniferists". On a mediocre site, the frustration of being unable to ripen even a tough vinifera, such as Chardonnay, despite all the efforts and good intentions can turn one against all vinifera varieties. Similarly, someone who has had considerable success with vinifera cannot understand why anyone in the area would bother with hybrids.

Look for a grower in your area who has had consistent success with any of the standard viniferas and then visit that vineyard. It will probably approach the ideal site specifications. A similar visit to one of the more vehement hybridists in the area will usually show that they have made more compromises in their site selection.

For those who have compromised with a less than ideal site, it may also

2

be practical to compromise with tougher and more disease resistant hybrid varieties. The more open the site and the more constant the summer breezes, provided also that one controls weeds and foliage so that air movement around the vines is not restricted, the easier it is to prevent diseases both during the summer and when the fruit is ripening.

Light Exposure

Grape vines will not tolerate shade. They may grow well and produce fine, large leaves, but production of fruit requires full sunlight. Partial shade will inhibit fruit bud formation and increasing shade will cause any flowers that may be produced to fall off. This can be seen in a vineyard where trees have been planted nearby. As the trees grow, shaded vines become increasingly unproductive.

Soil

Preferences are for moderately fertile soils, at least three feet deep if heavy or five feet deep if sandy. Soils should be well drained as the roots are damaged by a high water table.

If there is a question about a marginally wet area, dig a test hole four or five feet deep with a post-hole digger and see whether the water table rises during a wet period above the levels specified in the previous paragraph.

Other Factors

Nearby woods will generally support a considerable population of wild grape vines which serve as a ready source of various diseases and insects for the cultivated vines. An area noted for its deer hunting may require a fence to protect the vineyard. Woods also harbor smaller fauna that have a liking for grapes still too green for winemaking.

Nearby trees may grow up to shade the vines, perhaps trap cold air, compete for soil moisture and will harbor birds.

South facing slopes lengthen the season available while north facing slopes shorten it. This can be compensated for by planting late varieties on south slopes, early maturing ones on north slopes.

The favorable "moderating influence of a large body of water" does not apply to a small brook or pond, so don't rank this factor high in picking a site.

In regions where corn is a major crop, on sites within a half-mile of

utility or railroad rights-of-way, or even next door neighbors with mani-
cured lawns all pose a threat to vineyards from the drift of 2,4-D or
dicamba herbicides. The grapevine is especially sensitive to this class of
herbicides. Sometimes, through diplomacy or coercion, further damage
can be reduced, but when the source may be several miles away it can be
difficult to locate or control the damage.

Grapes have a wide ranging root system, easily a 30 foot radius. If
planted along the edge of a vegetable garden, the vines will flourish at the
expense of the vegetables. If the grapes are beside a lawn, fertilizer-her-
bicide combinations applied to the lawn may damage the vines.

Generally the nature of the site will determine the direction of the rows.
There are rarely strong objections to an aesthetic or convenient alignment.
Only on slopes too steep for a desirable site should rows run along the
contour. On rare occasions, east-west rows may promote better drying and
thus less disease, but more frequent sprays will readily compensate for
row orientation. If the site is oblong, you will find fewer end braces are
needed if the rows are run the long way.

CHOICE OF VARIETIES

It takes several decades of trial and error to sort through the available
varieties and at least a century to discover which particular variety is best
for each geographical area. European growers know which variety will be
most profitable in each area for a given style of wine. Californians are
approaching this state of knowledge. For the rest of the U.S., there is still a
long way to go. Part of the equation in the choice of varieties is the trade-off
between quality and quantity within each gradation of climate.

Three Types Of Grapes

The grower has the option to select from among three general types of
grapes the varieties which may be best adapted to his climate. These are
the time-tested American (labruscana) varieties, the hybrid direct producers (French hybrids) and the Old World varieties of Vitis vinifera. The
distinctions among these types are not as sharp as some have claimed.

Among the American varieties, there are some free of any labrusca
inheritance. All are derived, in part, from vinifera. A few are among the
most winter-hardy grapes. Most are relatively resistant to insects and diseases. Some recent American varieties were developed for Minnesota-type
climates, while others have tolerance to the extreme disease pressures of
Florida. Many of the varieties developed by American grape breeders in

the last quarter century are derived from or more closely resemble the inheritance of French hybrids than the older American varieties.

Among the French hybrids is a wide range of characteristics from almost wild to indistinguishable from vinifera in hardiness and pest susceptibility. The native American species in the inheritance of this group is complex and varied, but the varieties have been selected for minimum labrusca characteristics.

There are vinifera varieties that at best can produce only a common wine and even the viniferas of greatest repute, when grown outside their areas of climatic adaptation, may produce mediocre wines. One of the few generalizations that can be made about any of these groups is that the viniferas lack resistance to the insects and diseases endemic to eastern North America.

Based on the judgment of wines by the members of the American Wine Society in the National Amateur Wine Competitions, those made from vinifera (often with California-grown fruit) generally receive the Best of Show award, but not always. The lowly hybrid, DeChaunac, has received this respect. In the AWS Maryland competition, for which the individual scores of over 1,000 wine entries are available, the average scores for viniferas versus hybrids do not show marked differences.

In most areas with moderately severe climates, where diseases can be serious, or when an ideal site is not available, the planting of hybrids presents the grape grower with an acceptable option for producing estate wines. Unless there is certain knowledge that viniferas will either succeed or fail, both vinifera and hybrids should be tried and the grower permitted to make the decision based on performance of vines and quality of wine.

Muscadines

These are a fourth type of grape which is limited in adaptation to warmer, long season areas. Historically ill-used, frequently maligned, the muscadine, Vitis rotundifolia, is finally beginning to emerge as a grape capable of producing an acceptable table wine. In the past, the Scuppernong has served primarily as a carrier for sugar and brandy, an excuse for marketing alcohol under the tax classification of "wine".

So far as I can tell, no muscadine wines have been entered in the AWS wine contests for which I have rankings. However, several commercial muscadine wines have been judged in recent Wineries Unlimited competitions, not only in their own categories but also in direct competition with American wines where they were awarded several medals.

This emergence is the result of better varieties, as Carlos, Magnolia and Noble, and improved vinification methods pioneered at the Agricultural

Experiment Station laboratories in North Carolina and Mississippi. The muscadine, with tolerances to many pests, including Pierce's disease, and high productivity, is worthy of serious consideration in its area of adaptation.

Effect Of Climate

Climate affects both wine quality and vine survival. One must choose varieties that will ripen in the available growing season. One should also avoid varieties that ripen too early, in the heat of summer. Under hot conditions the delicate aromas of whites can be baked out and the wild taste of hybrids is accentuated. The wine quality of even the best vinifera is adversely affected by hot climates.

Most hybrids and several viniferas are sufficiently winter hardy to withstand all but the coldest areas of the East. Splitting of trunks results when low temperatures damage the tissues of non-dormant trunks followed by dehydration. Apparently some vinifera varieties are more apt to lose trunk dormancy during warm periods in the winter than are some of the hybrid and labruscana varieties. Therefore, they are more subject to this form of damage.

A second kind of winter damage results from loss of bud-dormancy. A period of a week at temperatures above 50°F can force growth activity in the buds of many viniferas and some hybrids, as Seibel 15062. These activated buds will be far more subject to damage by subsequent freezing.

A third type of winter damage is bud-kill of fully dormant buds at very low temperatures.

The riparia-derived hybrids are most hardy, followed by labruscana, French hybrids and vinifera, and varieties more frequently damaged by the variable winter temperatures of the mid-Atlantic States than by the more uniform cold of northern areas.

The distribution of rain during the ripening period also needs to be considered. The maturing berries of some varieties are subject to splitting following a rain, especially if they have previously been under a moisture stress. Fortunately, such varieties are few and this damage is infrequent on most varieties. Even the best spray program can fail to control diseases under some combinations of rain and humidity. One option available is to grow varieties which are resistant to the diseases present in the area.

Information On Locally Adapted Varieties

One must be very cautious about accepting either vine performance or wine quality from one area as recommendation for growing it in another area. Vignoles produces well and makes an excellent, balanced wine in New York, while in warmer areas of Maryland produces poorly and, even when sugars are as high as 25° Brix, the acid is often above 1.5%.

Beware of the Noah's Ark approach. You will learn little about the wine of each variety if your 100 vine vineyard has two vines each of 50 varieties. In any experimental planting, at least five and preferably ten vines each of a variety are needed to make a practical-sized sample of wine.

The recommendations of some of the states where the Agricultural Experiment Stations have several years of experience in grape or wine projects are helpful. AWS members who grow grapes in your area, local wineries and the regional grape wine organizations are excellent sources of information on variety performance.

One needs to be objective before accepting even these recommendations. The wine may be excellent, but how consistently does the variety produce and how much? Another wine sample may be poor, but was this the fault of the grape or the winemaker?

If grafted vines are to be grown, the choice becomes twice as difficult because a selection from among many available rootstock varieties must also be made. This is a Catch-22 situation. Before you can select the ideal rootstock, you must have discovered which qualities are required for each particular situation. The complexity of rootstock selection is noted in the Galet-Morton *Practical Ampelography.* The interim choice may well be what is available from the nursery. A choice of general-duty rootstocks or those that have not been a disaster in your area would be a fair guess for a first trial.

SOURCES OF PLANTS

The purchase of vines suitable for direct planting in the vineyard site can advance the first vintage by a year. Eventually, for economy or because certain vines may not be available from commercial sources, most growers will try propagating vines. Whether you purchase or propagate, someone must go through the following procedures.

Own-Rooted Cuttings

Slipshod work in the selection of mother vines is the primary source of variety mixtures and off-types. One must know that every vine from which propagation wood is taken is true-to-name.

Cuttings (see illustration) may be taken any time during the dormant season, but if they are not taken in the early fall they may be subject to bud damage from an unusually cold snap during the winter. The trade-off is that they must be stored until time to line them out after the last killing frost.

Cuttings can be stored in the old-fashioned method of tying and labeling with non-biodegradable wire and metal tags, and burying them vertically, bottom end up, at least four inches below the soil surface in well-drained soil. The reason for this orientation is that the spring warmth starts callusing and root growth before the buds begin to grow. If you remember where you buried them, they are carefully dug out and planted right side up in a nursery row.

The more modern storage involves bundles of cuttings, again tied and labeled with non-biodegradable materials, wrapped in moist newspaper or cloth, enclosed in a nonvented poly bag and held in a refrigerator or cool root cellar until planting time. A slight amount of freezing will not damage the wood. Bundles should be checked a couple of times to be sure they are not dry. Some mold may develop on the wrappings and wood, but this is generally not harmful.

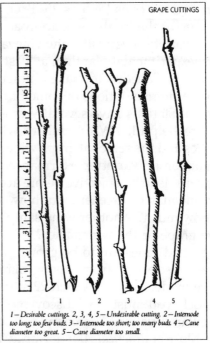

GRAPE CUTTINGS

1—Desirable cuttings. 2, 3, 4, 5—Undesirable cutting. 2—Internode too long; too few buds. 3—Internode too short; too many buds. 4—Cane diameter too great. 5—Cane diameter too small.

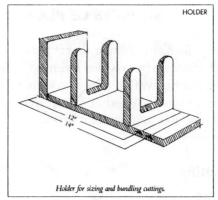

HOLDER

Holder for sizing and bundling cuttings.

In warmer areas, cuttings can be planted in the nursery in the fall. Where the soil can be expected to freeze to a depth of several inches, fall-planted cuttings may be heaved out of the ground. Where severe winter frosts are usual, the buds may be damaged. Thus, spring is the usual time to plant cuttings.

The percentage of successful cuttings depends on the variety, how well the cuttings were stored and the weather after planting. Seldom does one get 100%. Therefore, they are usually planted in a nursery for a year and the successful vines moved to the vineyard the next year.

Cuttings should be planted with two buds above ground. The buds below ground are a long-term insurance that if something damages the top, the vine may resprout from below ground and save vine replacement. If one can work the nursery soil to a sufficient depth, cuttings are best planted vertically. Planting them at an angle as great as 45 degrees is acceptable and less laborious.

Cuttings should be spaced about six inches apart in the nursery row. Placement further apart wastes space, closer makes it difficult to dig them without damage to the plants.

The better the soil preparation in the nursery, the better the growth of young vines. Use of chemical fertilizers in the nursery can be overdone very easily. Except on poor soils, hold any fertilizers until growth has started and do not fertilize late in the season.

Weed competition will slow growth of the cuttings. Frequent hoeing or planting cuttings through black plastic film or weed-preventive fabric will take care of weeds. The fabric material is more expensive, but does allow easier watering of young vines during a dry period. Judicious use of herbicides has sometimes worked well, but the variables of rainfall, soil type and movement of herbicides through the soil make this risky.

Frequently the shoots wil start growth before the roots are well established. Supplemental watering and perhaps some sort of protection against drying winds will give better survival of young plants. One can expect between 30 and 90% failure of cuttings, again depending on many factors. This rate of failure is the reason that direct planting of cuttings in the vineyard is not advised.

One wants good growth of young plants in the nursery, but if growth is encouraged by too much fertilizer too late in the summer, the wood will not mature properly and much of the new growth will be killed back in the fall.

With vines available at the site, digging and transplanting to the vineyard can be done at the most convenient time. Fall transplanting is recommended only in southern areas where the soil does not freeze more than an inch or two. Spring transplanting is done after the soil has thawed and before buds begin to grow. One is able to select a time when the soil is not too wet. The best vines can be selected, dug, trimmed and planted promptly without drying out. How much to cut back the roots and how to prune the tops is covered in Chapter 2.

Layering

Muscadines root from cuttings only with great difficulty. Mother vines are trained to bush out at ground level, shoots are placed to one side and the basal portions covered with soil. During the season, the shoots form roots under the soil. The following dormant season they can be transplanted to the vineyard.

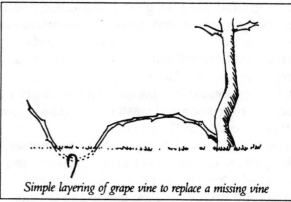

Simple layering of grape vine to replace a missing vine

Green Rooting

This specialized method works with most grapes. During the early part of the growing season, one or two bud cuttings with leaves attached are placed in containers in a cutting bed which has an automatic watermist system. The mist prevents the leaves from wilting until roots have formed. Rooting takes place in 3 or 4 weeks and the young plants can then be hardened for transplanting to the vineyard. The mist system must be failure-proof and requires considerable investment and attention. Mist propagation can be used in a greenhouse to root dormant cuttings or bench grafts. Such vines cannot be planted out until all danger of frost is past. The lead time on such green grafts is a year less than for regular bench grafted vines.

You may also be able to find a local greenhouse with a mist unit that would contract to start your vines.

Grafting

The use of rootstocks is preferred for vinifera varieties in all but sandy soils and may be useful for hybrids and even American varieties in some situations, as replanting a vineyard. The techniques are specialized and unless you plan to make a considerable investment in grafting tools, callus boxes with controlled temperature, and time, the purchase of grafted vines from commercial sources is suggested. For further information on grafting, see Chapter 3.

Purchase Of Vines

There is no change in the inherent nature of a variety caused by propagation in a climate different from that in which it will be grown. The hardiness of Chardonnay will be the same whether it was propagated in a frost-free area or in the coldest limits of its survival. But there is another factor that does argue for purchase of vines from a nearby source. Vines can carry diseases and some insects into areas where these pests are not normally present. These imported pests may die out under regular spray programs or surface only occasionally. Given a choice of sources, favor the nearby ones.

One of the most frustrating experiences of grape growing is to plant a vineyard only to find, after three years of patient cultivation, that the vines are not what was ordered. The liability of the nursery is only for the original cost of the vines. I do not know of any nursery that never makes a mistake. However, we growers now have available a method with which to identify most varieties during the first season. This is the "Practical Ampelography of Galet/Morton".

Another factor in the purchase of vines or of grafted vines, especially in large quantities, is that you may need to order them a year or two before you plant the vineyard.

ESTABLISHING THE VINEYARD

There are many facets in this phase of grape growing that will keep the grower busy over the period until the vines come into production.

Preplant Weed Control

Weeds are a discouraging feature of a vineyard. If time and equipment are available, cultivating the vineyard site for a year and plowing down a cover crop can improve the soil. Next best is to use some of the contact herbicides on spot infestations of weeds before planting. Otherwise, hoeing and very careful spot applications of herbicides after planting will be required.

Soil Analysis

If there is any indication that the soil fertility of the site is low or unbalanced, have an analysis made through your County Agent. Phosphorous, potassium and lime are more effective if worked into the soil before planting.

Laying Out And Planting

The vineyard should be staked out according to the site. Be sure you can get to both sides of each trellis row for spraying, mowing and harvesting. Straight rows are easier to brace than curves. The in-line posts in a curved row must be set much deeper to resist the pull of the wires as they are tightened.

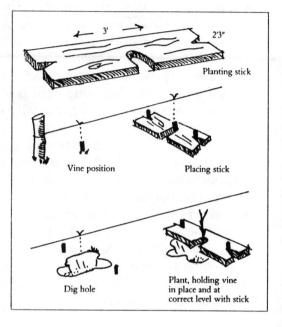

Planting stick

Vine position   Placing stick

Dig hole

Plant, holding vine in place and at correct level with stick

The distance between rows is usually determined by the equipment available. A small farm tractor needs nine to ten feet between rows for easy passage. Otherwise the minimum distance between rows is determined by the shadows cast by one row on the next. Three foot high rows can be three feet apart. Six foot high rows should be at least six feet apart.

If you are planting a quarter acre vineyard, you may eventually be forced to go to a small tractor and power sprayer. It would be better to space the rows eight or even ten feet apart as there is little gain in yield by closer spacing. Leave at least 15 to 20 feet at the ends of the rows for turning equipment and for vineyard maintenance.

When the spacing of rows is decided, mark and align where the posts will go. Preferred distance between posts is 18 to 24 feet with two vigorous or four weak-growing vines between. Vines can be planted beside concrete or metal posts. Wooden posts will eventually require replacement. If a vine is planted beside a post, there will be more damage to the roots than when planted away from from it.

Once the position of the posts is marked, the location of the vines has been determined. If the soil has been prepared by cultivation, it is a matter of digging holes and firming in the vines. Sight along the row as you plant to be sure each vine is within an inch or so of the center line. A vine that is off-center tends to get in the way of later operations. A planting board, illustrated, can help in aligning vines.

If the vines are to be planted in sod, not a preferred method, it is possible to spray an herbicide, such as Roundup, over a strip or in an area two or three feet across where each vine is to be planted. This must be done three or four weeks before planting to have time to be effective in killing the sod. This is less laborious than removing the sod for each vine space.

If vines are to planted in a heavy soil, it may seem helpful to dig an oversize hole for each vine and refill around the roots with a nice rich compost rather than with the original soil. This is not worth the effort. The root system is encouraged to develop within the confines of the hole and excessive moisture may be held within the original hole to the detriment of the young vine.

Even in lighter soils, adding compost to the planting hole may discourage the preferred wide-ranging root system that gives the vine its ability to seek out nutrients and moisture from a large volume of soil.

Digging more than a dozen planting holes is a major chore in heavy or stony soils. For more vines than this, see if you can find and hire a local farmer who has a large tractor and subsoiler which can be run along the center of the rows to be planted.

Trenching or deep plowing to a depth of two or four feet may sometimes encourage early growth, but within three years the original soil structure will be re-established. The considerable effort involved is seldom worthwhile and under some conditions, more harm than good results.

To Stake Or Trellis

As soon as the vines begin to grow, they should be trained vertically. This means a four or five foot stake for each vine, or preferably, that the permanent trellis posts be installed and at least the lower wire put up. If vines are not carefully trained in the first season, there will be unsightly crooked trunks that get in the way of later operations.

The training process — select the best one or two shoots and remove unwanted side shoots — is illustrated in Chapter 2.

Choice Of Posts

For five to ten vines in short rows, sturdy metal posts, not the economy line, are sufficient. They can be driven with a sledge or post pounder. They will eventually be weakened by rust at the ground line, but replacement is relatively simple.

The nearest to a permanent post is reinforced concrete, if you can find them or afford them. If you expect to be growing grapes for a long time, they are probably the best investment in trellises. Another elite style of trellis post is 2" galvanized pipe. A recent product of the recycling revolution is an extruded sawdust/plastic post which promises to be better than it sounds.

There are many kinds of wooden posts on the market. Treated pine, the tapered kind, are reasonably priced and have a good life expectancy. Veneer cores, which can be recognized as the perfect cylinders that are left over from plywood production, are cheaper, but begin to fail in a couple of years. This is because the anti-rot treatment does not take as well and because some are mechanically weak.

There are several natural woods, Virginia cedar, catalpa, osage orange and black locust, that can be used for trellis posts. The osage orange needs a couple of years of aging or will sprout out into a forest. Black locust needs to be selected for good heart wood. A nice straight regrowth sapling, even five or six inches in diameter, can rot out in five years. Split locust heartwood posts last 50 years.

Whichever kind of wooden post you use, expect to start replacing a few posts within five years and perhaps five percent each year after 15 years.

Setting Wooden Posts

Unless you can hire a tractor-mounted postdriver with a skilled crew, two pieces of equipment are needed. These are a post-hole digger (auger or knuckle-buster) and a mushroom tamper. Set the end posts and then dig the post holes, line up and tamp the inline posts. The base and top must both be aligned and the tops of uniform height above ground level. One can go through after setting posts and even off the tops with a chain saw.

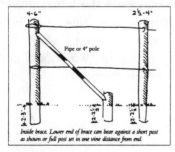
Inside brace. Lower end of brace can bear against a short post as shown or full post set in one vine distance from end.

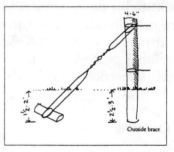
Outside brace

In heavy soils, setting the intermediate posts two feet in the ground is sufficient. In a sandy loam or sand, two and a half feet is preferred.

End Posts

Size and bracing of end posts depend on the length of the row. If the row is less than 50 feet long, a six to eight inch diameter post set three feet deep may hold without bracing. Rows more than 50 feet will require an inside diagonal brace or an outside stay to a soil anchor. For a soil anchor, steel screw augers are available for a price. Just as good is a loop of heavy galvanized wire stapled to the post and around a concrete block or two foot long piece of locust buried horizontally about one and a half to two feet deep. Slack is taken up by twisting the two sides of the loop together after the anchor is set and tamped.

Wire

Galvanized, soft-annealed steel wire is the usually recommended style. The thicker the galvanized layer, the longer the wire will last. For rows less than 50 feet, 11 or 12 gauge is sufficient. For longer rows, 9 gauge is a good investment.

Crimped wire may be good for commercial vineyards, but is not as easy to install and may be difficult to find. Plastic filaments have not proven satisfactory in vineyards. They are difficult to tighten and very apt to be cut during pruning or harvest.

There are many ways to tighten the wires: ready-made units, turn-buckles, eye-bolts or homemade devices. Not recommended are the type that attach along the wire and are twisted to take up slack. These crimp the wire and weaken it, es-pecially after several years of weathering.

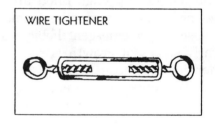

WIRE TIGHTENER

At one end-post, the wire can be run twice around the post, twisted and stapled. At the other end-post, it can be attached to an eye-bolt or run through a hole and around a wire tightener. If a turnbuckle is used, the wire is fixed to both end-posts. On the intermediate posts, staples are preferable to holes through each post because of the difficulties involved with replacing a defective post. Staples should not be driven tight so that the wire tension can be adjusted.

Some provision is needed, especially in colder areas, for slacking tension during winter. Any system that does not allow for this will put an undue strain on the trellis.

Various commercial devices are available and a Wire-Vise fitting may be preferable for hard annealed wire. For soft annealed wire, an inexpensive tightener can be made from scrap half-inch iron pipe. These have been effective for trellis runs up to several hundred feet. Hard annealed wire does not work well with this device as it tends to break when bent.

The number and general placement of wires depends on the training system and height of the posts. Several of these are shown in Chapter 2.

If chemical weed control is to be used under the vines, the lowest wire should be two and a half feet to three feet high to reduce the chance of damage to vine foliage.

If multiple arm Kniffin training is used, in which new shoots are tied along the wires, spacing between wires of less than one and a half feet will result in excessive shading and negligible increase in yield.

Weed Control After Planting

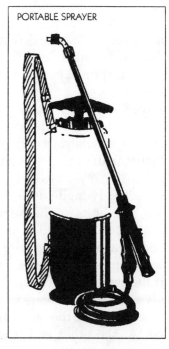

PORTABLE SPRAYER

Weeds must be controlled, especially during the first couple of years. A three foot square of black plastic or other weed-suppressing material around the base of each vine is one method that saves much hoeing. Edges are held down with soil, stones or nails pushed through into the soil. Grass clippings piled around the young vines may smother some weeds.

Use of pre-emergent hebicides in the early stages of growth is risky. Contact herbicides, those that kill established weeds as opposed to preventing germination of weed seeds, can be useful if care is taken. A paper milk carton, open at both ends, placed over each vine and held in place with a stake immediately after planting will protect it from contact herbicides. It will also serve to shade the young vines and may protect against rabbits. Alternately, a metal or cardboard shield on the end of a handle can be held in front of a vine while treating adjacent weeds.

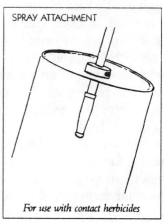

SPRAY ATTACHMENT

For use with contact herbicides

For instance, an empty coffee can is attached to the end of the spray wand as shown in the sketch. For a controlled application of herbicide, even in a gale, place the open end of the can over the weed in question and pull the trigger. The shield allows one to use contact herbicides much closer to the vines without as much chance of damage to the vine as there is far less spray drift. It is great for soaking taller weeds. Lower the shield over the taller weeds with a circular motion until the open end is almost at ground level and then pull the trigger.

Cutting the round hole in the can is done with the proper sized hole saw or a drill and small tin snips. How to attach the can to the spray wand is solved with an electrical cable clamp. Either a BX or Romex clamp will do. The size is determined by the diameter of the spray nozzle or whether the nozzle can be removed in order to slip the clamp onto the wand.

You may want to apply flat black paint to the exposed end of the shield so that sunlight does not reflect back into your eyes and make the weeds more difficult to see.

One final step is put up some sort of permanent row numbers and variety labels.

Cropping

All fruit that sets on vines the first year must be removed. The only reason to leave a single cluster on a vine the second year is to help identify off types or mixtures in the planting. Only after vine foliage has filled the trellis, hopefully by the end of the second season, can a crop be produced safely. Both French hybrid and vinifera vines are subject to damage if cropped too soon or too heavily. A crop taken too soon will be paid for in weakened vines and smaller crops in later years.

VINEYARD MANAGEMENT

This includes the operations required to maintain a mature vineyard and decisions which balance the current crop of fruit against the survival of vines to produce the next year's crop. This year's crop must be ripened, yet the vine must also be prepared to withstand the cold of winter and to initiate fruitful buds for the following year.

In general, the sequence is to encourage growth early in the season, control crop size, maintain sufficient effective foliage throughout the growing season and, by reducing available nitrogen after midseason, to encourage good wood maturity and carbohydrate reserves in the vines before frost removes the foliage.

Clean Cultivation

The preferred method for handling the space between trellis rows in many commercial vineyards is an annual sequence of several cultivations followed by the planting of a cover crop in the late summer. The main role of the cover crop is to reduce available nitrogen and hasten wood maturity. The necessary equipment is often not practical for the home vineyard and the small grower can readily compensate for most advantages of the annual cultivation cycle.

Grass Centers

A permanent sod of shallow-rooted grasses, such as blue grass or creeping fescue, is more practical than clean cultivation for the small vineyard. Sod should be solid enough to prevent broadleaf weeds from becoming established. Tall fescue seldom forms a thick turf and with a deeper root system requires more frequent mowing than shallower rooted grasses. Aside from the need for mowing, grass centers compete for water and soil nutrients, and may permit the buildup of destructive insects. Several broadleaf weeds, as dandelion, can serve as the source for tomato and tobacco ring-spot viruses that can damage many grape varieties.

A strip two to three feet wide under the vines should be kept free of weeds. Black plastic probably has more more disadvantages (it is difficult to hold in place, must be replaced after a couple of years and may harbor mice) than advantages (does keep down weeds, retains moisture, traps some destructive insects). A thick (three to six inch deep) layer of straw or grass clippings under the row of vines will discourage many weeds. But only when the soil under the vines is bare, will heat accumulate in the soil that can reradiate to protect the young shoots. If the mulch is in place during the spring, or if there is a layer of weeds under the vines, the risk of frost damage to the young growth is increased.

Perhaps the easiest method is a combination of hoeing and chemical weed control. A combination of pre-emergent and contact herbicides will reduce the amount of hand labor required. After a couple of years, the weed population will stabilize at a very low level. Seeds, wind-borne and from the grass centers, will continue to make a weed control program necessary.

Fertilizer

Applications of fertilizer should be based on soil or petiole analyses available through your County Agent. There are excellent color photographs of various nutrient deficiencies in the California Priced Publication 4087.

Training And Pruning

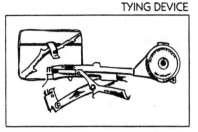

TYING DEVICE

These are well covered in Chapter 2. Crop control is again stressed because it is the primary cause of poor vine growth, inferior wine and winter kill of vines.

The disposal of prunings is an annual chore. Mechanical rakes, brush hogs and such heavy-duty machines have a place in large commercial vineyards. The small grower may want to recycle some of the wood as cuttings for vineyard expansion or sale. Some can be cut into fagots for starting the fire the following fall.

Removal of prunings from the vineyard to a distant compost pile, especially old dead trunks, is recommended as a good way to prevent the buildup of Eutypia dieback disease.

Vine trunks can be tied up with strong cord or plastic ties, leaving enough slack so the trunks or arms are not girdled as they grow. New growth can be tied up out of the way of herbicide sprays with a tying device or light string (see illustration).

Shoots that grow in full light will be more fruitful. When pruning, one prefers to retain those from upper levels of the trellis. If you can identify early in the growing season those shoots that arise from the best location on the trunk for the next year's fruiting wood, position them for better exposure to light.

If a vine is undercropped, judicious removal of the terminal foot or tipping of vigorous shoots will keep the vine in better balance and may improve fruit quality. Such tipping may be required several times during the season.

Crop Control

Removal of some clusters is necessary on many large-clustered varieties. If done before blossoming, the remaining clusters will be even larger. A combination of removal of clusters before bloom and after setting will give an optimum control of crop size. This allows one to underprune vines so that the vigor is increased without loss of crop quality or danger of vine damage.

When you go through the vineyard thinning clusters, a trick that can be most helpful at harvest time is to position the remaining clusters so that they are not tangled across a shoot or wire. When they hang free, they will be in a better position for spraying and much easier to harvest. The time it takes to do this will be saved at the time of harvest.

Pests And Other Troubles

There are several fungus diseases that can result in a major crop loss or reduced wine quality. Some of these diseases are restricted to certain geographical areas.

Powdery mildew is an exception, being present in all areas, both dry and humid. The damage is related primarily to the susceptibility of the varieties grown. Most American varieties and some French hybrids are sufficiently resistant that no special control measures are needed.

In cooler, humid areas, the major diseases are downy mildew and phomopsis twig and leaf blight.

In intermediate areas, black rot, bitter rot and Pierce's disease are considered most damaging.

Downy mildew can show up in all areas during cooler, wet weather.

Eutypia die-back (the more destructive phase of the disease formerly called deadarm) may be a problem in all areas on older vines, especially where fungicides are applied infrequently. Train vines with two trunks so that when a diseased trunk must be removed, there will not be a one or two year loss of crop.

Crown gall appears to be related to the wound callus that forms following frost cracking or splitting of trunks. Some vines may carry the bacteria which cause this disease and thus be more subject to damage. Multiple trunk training allows one to replace severely damaged trunks with a minimum of crop loss.

Botrytis, the gray mold fungus, is widely distributed and damage is related to both wet seasons and relative susceptibility of the varieties grown. There are now several fungicides registered for control of this disease. Most state spray schedules indicate which materials for botrytis control best fit in with the effective control of other diseases and specify the generally critical timing of sprays.

There are probably another dozen fungus diseases which may show up under unusual conditions or seasons. Most will be sucessfully suppressed by a regular fungicide spray program.

With many of these diseases, there is a buildup of the damage over a period of two or more years. Good control each year will reduce the problem for the following year. A valuable help is "Compendium of Grape Diseases" by Pearson and Goheen (see Appendix).

Because of the variability between climates, the differences in susceptibility of varieties and differences between growing seasons, no single spray schedule will be practical for all areas or vineyards. A good starting place is the spray schedules published by the State Agricultural Experiment Stations, either from your own state or one from a nearby state.

There are many more insects than diseases of the vine. Again, some are geographically limited, and some will build up over a period of two or more years. The standard spray schedule will give adequate control, although special sprays may be needed for unusual outbreaks.

The two or three years needed to establish a vineyard gives one time to learn the local diseases and the appropriate preventative sprays. An exception is a planting of any variety susceptible to powdery mildew. Failure to control this disease will so weaken the young vines that they may be subject to winter kill.

There are several types of leaf symptoms that may be confused with fungus diseases.

Herbicides can produce malformed leaves or veinal yellowing. Minor element deficiencies (as iron or magnesium) can cause yellowing or vein banding. Some virus diseases can cause a variety of yellowing, vein banding or leaf distortion. A normal senescence of leaves formed early in the season can occur by midseason, due mainly to shading by younger foliage and lateral growth of the shoots. Finally, malformed or torn leaves at the base of shoots can result from low winter temperatures.

A dead vine presents a real problem; the corpse is there, but the culprit may be difficult to identify. The vine that resprouts from the base after the top has died may represent an almost lethal effect of the same culprit. The commonest cause is overcropping. What was the sugar level of the fruit? If less than 18%, overcropping is a good possibility. Low winter temperatures, variable winter temperatures, loss of foliage from diseases about the time of harvest, grape root borer (warmer areas), Pierce's disease (areas with mild winters only), lightning damage, too much fertilizer on small vines, wrong spray material, wet feet, phylloxera (on heavy soils), nematodes (light soils), Eutypa (generally the typical fungus structures can be seen) are among the long and varied list of possibilities, but **GREED** is the worst killer of all and the easiest to control.

Birds, Etc.

A most frustrating experience is to do everything correctly and just before a fine harvest to have birds destroy the crop. Netting the vineyard is both costly and laborious, but may be necessary to allow full ripening of the crop.

A vineyard is also a favorite grazing area for deer. An expensive fence will work; repellents (proprietary products, bags of human hair, lion dung, bars of smelly soap, etc.) may work if the feeding pressures are not great.

Rabbits can cut off young vine trunks and later eat low hanging clusters on mature vines. A two-foot high chicken wire fence will exclude them, provided you have the bottom edge well fastened to the soil surface.

Possums and raccoons are a perennial problem for many growers. They do not respect the sort of fences that keep out rabbits. A couple of our member growers have reported good success with an electric fence strung at about six inches above ground level.

ORGANICALLY GROWN GRAPES?

It is no problem to grow organically just about anywhere.

The definition of "grapes" is broad enough to include the tough, inedible, undrinkable wild species of Vitis. Nor does the statement assure one of a crop every year even with the wild grapes.

As the definition of grape is narrowed to varieties which produce fruit increasingly suitable for wine, the genetic content from V. vinifera increases and so does susceptibility to insects and fungal diseases. Those who would grow only varieties best suited for wine must either forsake the environment or move to an irrigated region. A compromise between pesticide use and wine quality is available in the hybrid varieties which require less pesticides. For both, a good vineyard site, skilled vineyard management and extra hand labor can reduce the need for pesticide use.

Those who would forgo all pesticides must be willing and able to adapt their winemaking practices to compensate for the remarkable acid levels, low sugars and peculiar flavors of our native species. Perhaps genetic engineering will someday protect a Cabernet Sauvignon with the tough epidermis of a V. berlandieri, but until such time a trade-off between variety and pest tolerance is the only option.

HARVESTING

Determining the time to harvest is a confrontation between the attitudes of the "grower" and the "winemaker". The grower wants to pick as early as possible before rots, birds, raincracking or frost decimate the crop. The winemaker wants fully ripened, well-balanced fruit appropriate to the style of wine he envisions.

As berries mature, there is more than color development and softening of the pulp. Three other changes are underway that affect the wine produced. So long as the foliage is healthy and the sun shines, the sugar levels increase. At warm temperatures, the acids in the green fruits are respired, with malic acid levels decreasing more rapidly than tartaric acid and the pH rises. Finally, in an interaction between available sugars (from photosynthesis) and temperature, the *desirable aromas* characteristic of the variety will develop, increase to a peak and then may fall, leaving less desirable ones to predominate.

In a climate that is relatively consistent from year to year, these three characteristics develop in a fairly consistent relationship so that the optimum time for harvest can be determined by measuring a single characteristic, or by the more elegant sugar/acid ratio based on two measurements that will predict with good reliability the fruit maturity.

For climates with irregular patterns of temperature and sunshine, the relationships among these three characteristics will vary independently. Cool, sunny days can result in high levels of both sugar and acid. Warm cloudy days may cause a drop in acid without accumulation of sugar.

Because both acid level and aroma development are primarily temperature-moderated while fruit sugar is the result of insolation and the ratio of crop size to effective leaf area, the measurement of total acid, titratable acid and/or pH of the fruit is a better index of overall maturity than sugar level. Only experience over a wide variation of seasons can give a full appreciation of when the varietal aromas are at their optimum.

Of these characteristics, it is easiest for the winemaker to correct a low sugar level. For the home winemaker, the option to add sugar as needed is a positive advantage and one that is used when necessary throughout the world.

The desirable acid level depends on the style of wine to be made. Fresh, fruity wines, red or white, are protected against a malolactic (secondary) fermentation. Therefore, a starting level of about 0.75% is preferred. If a solid red or white wine is to be made, acid levels of about 1.0% will usually drop to acceptable levels as the result of a secondary fermentation. Musts above 1.2% acid may be too high to undergo secondary fermentation without such manipulations as blending or acid-stripping of a portion of the must.

The 5 to 10 ml. sample of fruit needed for an acid titration should not be considered too costly a percentage of even the smallest home vineyard crop when you realize the improvement in wine quality that results from properly matured fruit. There is too often a green-grape taste in both homemade and commercial wines. This taste differs from the herbaceous taste of too-hard pressed whites or stemmy reds and is not readily overcome by the techniques of the winemaker.

There is another small group of off-flavors that relate directly to the fruit, rather than to the fermentation. A small percentage of bitter rot-infected berries will give the wine a truly nasty taste. Powdery mildew infected berries can give wine a musty taste. If a few berries are damaged by birds or rain cracking and have fermented for a day or more in the vineyard, the level of acetic acid they carry into the wine may be both noticeable and objectionable. Prevention of all such diseased or damaged berries is an ideal goal that may seldom be achieved in the vineyard.

If and when these potential hazards to the wine do appear at the time of harvest, their ill effects can be reduced by careful removal of damaged berries. The difference between a common wine and a good one depends on the recognition of and care taken in discarding damaged berries before they are crushed. This one laborious step is the most significant advantage the small winemaker has over a commercial operation.

THE GREAT INTERNATIONAL GRAPE LOTTERY

The longer a particular variety is cultivated, the more desirable mutations appear and are propagated as "clones". With machine harvesting, commercial growers have far less chance of finding these interesting and valuable changes. The home grower who becomes more familiar with each vine still has a chance to detect such sports. Larger clusters, more open clusters (less susceptible to rots), different color fruit, better vigor, better crop size, are the kinds of changes one may be lucky enough to spot. The chance of finding better disease or insect resistance is slight. One does need to watch out that a "sport" may be another variety, compliments of the nurseryman, or a chance seedling.

Even a sport that appears as a single cluster on one shoot may be "captured" by propagating from the buds opposite, above or below that cluster. One needs to prove the real value of such a sport by growing several vines over a couple of vegetative propagations, a matter of several years, in order to demonstrate that it is preferable to the original type.

CHAPTER TWO

BASIC GUIDE TO PRUNING

By John R. McGrew, PhD.

INTRODUCTION

THIS CHAPTER is intended primarily for the amateur wine maker who grows hybrid direct producers (French-American hybrids) or who is experimenting with viniferas under less than ideal climates. Because a quarter acre should produce the legal limit of 200 gallons, I have suggested several techniques which may not be practical in larger, commercial vineyards.

This chapter is intended to be a brief guide to a single phase of viticulture. To clarify what can be a confusing subject, we offer an occasional definition or rule of thumb.

1. There are two kinds of buds on a grapevine, those that give rise to shoots that bear fruit and those that do not.

2. Buds formed on wood of the previous season's growth are fruitful buds.

3. Training puts the crop in an economical and convenient position.

4. A renewal spur gives rise to a vigorous shoot that will be retained for the fruiting cane the following year.

5. Pruning controls the size of the crop.

6. Fruit production is competitive with vegetative growth.

Pruning

The most perplexing task of the beginning grape grower is pruning the vines. Prune too lightly and both vine and fruit quality suffer from overcropping. An unpruned vine may have 10 to 100 times more flowers than it can possibly ripen. Prune too severely and the yield is reduced, the vine is difficult to manage, and vine structure may be less than optimum the following year. Further, the optimum pruning level is dependent on the unique conditions of each vineyard.

Fortunately, the line between under- and over-pruning is not a highwire balancing act. One has both leeway and techniques to compensate for misjudgements. With an understanding of what the vine can do and with some experience, the psychological hazards of pruning can be reduced to pleasant outdoor excercise.

Training

A training system is more than the static appearance of the pruned vine as illustrated in books. Just as significant is the management of shoots, including placement of fruit, leaf exposure, and special attention to renewal shoots. Two training systems may look identical at the beginning of the season, but once growth begins, may take on very different forms.

Choice of a particular training system depends on the growth habits of the variety, economic consideration of trellis construction, and labor available for pruning, cluster removal and positioning of summer tying of shoots.

Plan Ahead

If there is a secret to pruning, it is one so obvious that it is assumed in most instructions. You are told to leave renewal spurs in appropriate places when you prune in the dormant season. You are told to position the shoots, which will be used as fruiting canes the following year, for best exposure to light so that buds will be fully fertile.

The unstated role for the grower is to look critically at each vine several times during the growing season. Identify and "train" the fruiting wood for the following year. Remove excess or poorly positioned shoots, encourage growth if necesary by removal of clusters and lateral growth, and tie up for good light exposure. If this is done successfully, the decisions of where to cut have been made before the previous crop is harvested. Such vines are easy to prune.

STARTING THE VINEYARD

Before one can control the size or placement of the crop, the vine must be established. During the first 2 years, vines are handled similarly regardless of variety or training system to be used.

Rooted vines should be planted as early as practical in the spring. Fall planting is recommended only in areas where winter freezing is not severe. Newly set vines may be damaged by dry weather or drying winds before they have developed a good root system. Watering may be essential for survival.

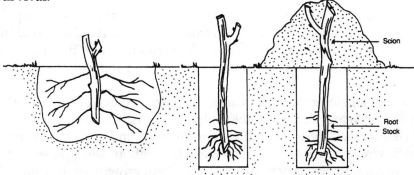

Figure 1 – Planting

As many roots as possible on dormant nursery vines should be retained if one is able to dig a large hole and spread out the roots carefully. They should be cut back to fit a smaller hole if an auger or post-hole digger is used, rather than stuffed into the hole. The top is cut back to 2 buds. Depth at which an own-rooted vine is planted is not critical. The graft-union of a grafted vine (right) should be just above ground level and should be hilled over with soil, sand, or peat, or protected with an open-ended cylinder until a strong new shoot has formed. When the mound is removed, any roots from the scion must be removed.

Single Trunks

For most situations a vine with a single trunk is easier to handle. During the first growing season, retain only the straightest, most vigorous shoot and train it up a stake with enough ties to assure it will remain straight. To encourage strong growth, remove all other shoots that may sprout from the base of the vine (Fig. 2,b-c). Side branches will grow from the bud at the base of each new leaf along the retained shoot. Remove all except three or four of these laterals at the level of each wire (Fig. 2 d).

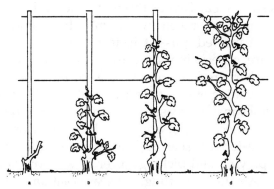

Figure 2 – First years growth

Multiple Trunks

For some varieties and under some climates, two or more trunks provide insurance against loss of production from damage to trunks by cold injury, Eutypia die-back or crown gall. Multiple trunks may also provide a means to compensate for winter injury to buds of vinifera and more tender hybrid varieties.

Whether single or multiple trunks are used, the maximum growth during the first year will be possible only if the trellis is installed before the new shoots reach the level of the wires. Pinching and tying should be done on each vine every two or three weeks throughout the first season. The trellis wires are necessary to support the lateral growth for maximum light exposure.

Prompt removal of suckers and laterals is desirable. Until they have formed several mature leaves, they drain energy from the vine. If removed while still young, they are easily snapped off. Such early training of a vine can advance the first full crop by at least a year.

CULTURAL PRACTICES

FIRST GROWING SEASON

Except on the poorest soils, elimination of weed or grass competition will do more to improve vine growth than generous amounts of fertilizer. Chemical herbicides should be used only with caution on young vines. Hand hoeing, black plastic, mulch or grass clippings are the best methods available. A rotary tiller should not be used within a foot or two of a young vine.

If you plan to cultivate between trellis rows, start cultivating the first season. This will cut surface roots before the vine can become dependent on them. Do not increase the depth of cultivation once a level has been established. Two or three inch depth is sufficient if cultivation is frequent enough to prevent weeds from becoming well established.

A mowed grass strip in the middle competes with the vines for moisture, especially if deep rooted grasses predominate. Insect pests may also be harbored. In areas where spring frosts may damage young growth, the insulating effect of grass or mulch in the vineyard and especially under the vines may increase the amount of frost damage.

If these do not appear to be major worries and if you have water available for dry seasons, the grass middles minimize erosion and do make spraying and picking easier in wet weather.

Any insect or fungus disease that damages an appreciable portion of the leaf area will slow growth of the vines. This is the time to learn to recognize the various problems and determine when and with what materials to control them. It is excellent practice to prevent the build-up of diseases in a young vineyard.

Dormant Pruning

Whenever a vine is pruned, make sure the wood and buds that are to be retained are alive. Generally, the terminal portion of a shoot will not mature and will be winter-killed. The wood of the live portion of a cane is firm and springy, and the cut end of live wood is green. It is rare, but not impossible, that the buds may be damaged even though the wood is still green. Damaged buds are brown in the center when cut.

Much concern has been wasted over the natural phenomenon of "bleeding" of late-pruned vines. Indeed, late pruning will delay bud-break and thus reduce the chance of frost damage to young shoots.

When to Prune

Vines may be pruned at any time from leaf-drop until budburst. Pruning before mid-winter presents a risk if low temperatures damage more buds than anticipated. Pruning after buds have started to swell is time consuming because considerable care must be taken not to break off buds when pulling wood or positioning canes.

A compromise is to rough prune during milder days in fall and winter, leaving two or three times the amount of wood necessary. To do this, one makes the major decisions on preferred canes and pulls off most of the excess wood. Avoid pruning during freezing weather as the wood may be brittle. Once rough pruned and the vines are cut loose from the wires, trellis repairs can be made. Then when bud burst approaches, do the final pruning, tighten the wires, and tie up the vine.

Age of Wood

Throughout this book, a distinction is made between "Wood of the previous season" and older wood. The wood of the previous season has smooth bark and obvious buds below which can be found the scar where the leaf was borne. The bark on older wood is shaggy and stringy and buds are not so obvious.

The bark at the base of last year's wood that has grown vigorously may be somewhat roughened and often has well developed lateral branches.

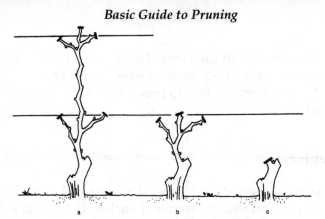

Figure 3 – Pruned, start of second year.

To Cut-Back or Not

If you have controlled weeds, tended the young vines and put in the trellis the first growing season, the vines should have made enough growth so that they can be pruned as shown in figure 3. On the left (a) is four-arm Kniffin training, and center (b) is Keuka high-renewal.

The many buds and starch stored in the stems gets these vines off to a rapid and strong growth in the second season. The shoot from each bud will usually produce flower clusters which must be removed. It may require two or three minutes per vine for this necessary chore.

If, and only if, there has been winter damage to the stem, or the vines have not made good growth for whatever reason, or the task of removing clusters is not practical, the alternative is to cut back to two buds (fig. 3c) and return to the conditions shown in figure 2a. To cut back this severely when not really necessary will delay crop production, but the new growth the second year should be far more vigorous than from newly planted vines. If you cut back to two buds, you must repeat the suckering, tying and training. Crop control the following year will be achieved through a combination of pruning and cluster removal.

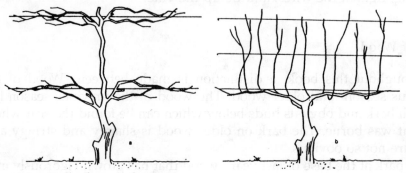

Figure 4 – End of second year.

Figure 4 (a & b) shows the vines at the end of the second growing season and before pruning. During the summer, tie the shoots along or up the wires, and remove all flower clusters to permit maximum vine growth. Remove all shoots that develop from buds other than those on the spurs shown in Figure 3. This will require less effort than removing the 2 or 3 clusters that may form on each new shoot.

How to prune this vine for fruit production in the next growing season is covered in Figure 9, after we explain which buds are fruitful.

FRUIT PRODUCTION

If a vine is sufficiently vigorous to fill the trellis at the end of the second growing season, one may plan for a small crop (perhaps 25% as many fruiting buds as a mature vine will carry) in the third growing season. The goal now changes from establishing a sturdy vine to the production of a controlled quantity of fruit. Where does the fruit come from?

Figures 5 through 8 are of a small portion of a mature vine. They show the sequence of fruit formation, the roles of the 2 kinds of buds, and demonstrate the annual cycle of growth and the pruning by which the crop size is controlled. In practice, several buds are retained on each fruiting cane and 2 buds on each renewal spur.

1. **There are 2 kinds of buds on a grapevine, those that give rise to shoots that bear fruit and those that do not.**

2. **Buds formed on wood of the previous season's growth are fruitful buds. (Exceptions are noted after Figure 5).**

This relationship to age of wood on which buds are borne holds true for most American varieties and many viniferas. On some French hybrids, such as DeChaunac, as much as half the crop may arise from buds on 2 year or older wood. Conversely, many buds on 1 year old wood that developed under low light intensities, as on shoots at the bottom of the vine or on overcropped vines, may be unfruitful.

Figure 5 – Types of buds shown before growth starts in the spring. The main trunk is several years old, spur "2" is 2 years old. Spur "1" was produced the previous growing season, therefore bud "a" is fruitful. Bud "b" is on 2 year old wood and bud "c" on mature wood. Because the "b" and "c" are on old wood, generally neither are fruitful.

Figure 6 – Early growth.

During the growing season bud "a" grows into a shoot with fruit clusters, tendrils, leaves, and a new bud at the base of each leaf. The number of fruit clusters on each shoot varies according to variety, but the average number is 3 per shoot. Buds "b" and "c" may grow into shoots with tendrils, leaves, and new buds, but generally have no fruit.

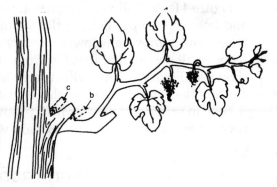

Figure 7 – Mature

Later in the growing season, some of the new buds on these shoots grow into branch shoots. Because these branch shoots, as "d", are from this season's growth, they generally do not produce flowers. A secondary bud will form at the base of every shoot. If bud "e" were to grow (the secondary bud of fruitful bud "d"), it can in some varieties produce flowers and fruit.

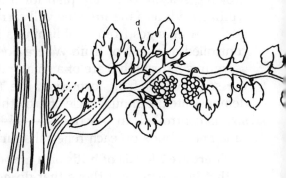

Figure 8 – After leaf fall.

After harvest and leaf-fall, there is extensive wood present that was produced during the now previous growing season. Essentially all of the many buds on this wood are fruitful. One of several choices is shown on where to prune to retain a single fruitful bud and thus return to the conditions in Figure 5. In practice, several fruitful buds are retained on a fruiting cane and the cane with sufficient buds and best placement would be selected. Buds on canes of moderate vigor that were not shaded during the previous season will be more fruitful.

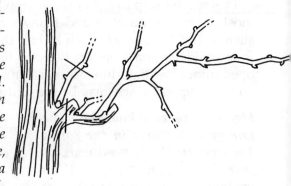

TRAINING

3. Training puts the crop in an economical and convenient position.

The number of fruitful buds to leave is discussed in the following section on pruning. Where to leave them so that the fruit is borne in a convenient place for spraying and harvesting, and so that the time and labor for pruning and tying are kept low is determined by the training method selected.

No matter what variety of training method is used, you should retain buds specifically for fruiting and buds specifically to produce the fruiting wood for the following year. The latter buds are generally those on renewal spurs.

The length of the fruiting cane is determined by the number of fruitful buds to be retained. The cane may be of any length from short, sometimes called spur pruned, to long.

4. A renewal spur gives rise to a vigorous shoot this year that will be retained for the fruiting cane the following year.

The renewal spur is generally pruned to 2 buds. Because there are only two shoots formed, they will usually be more vigorous than shoots on the fruiting canes and thus more suitable in the year following. The buds on the renewal spur are fruitful. If the renewal shoot is vigorous, it can be allowed to fruit. If it has not made good growth by mid-summer, removal of the green fruit clusters will better ensure a good fruiting cane for the following year. The renewal shoots should receive preferential positions in full sunlight.

There are hundreds of training methods described in the viticulture literature. A single training method may appear in many areas of the world under several names. Differences may be no more than trellis configuration, number of trunks, or position in which fruiting canes are tied. We show only 4 general types popular in this country. Three of these could be used on a single stretch of trellis, or one can convert from one to another without loss of crop. The Munson requires a different trellis.

Kniffin Training

The concept of long, horizontal fruiting canes was re-discovered when an apple tree fell on one vine in Wm. Kniffin's Hudson Valley vineyard in 1850. The flattened vine was the most productive in the vineyard. This training system (Figure 9) or one of its many variants is standard for most American varieties and many of the French hybrids. Most varieties, including viniferas can be adapted to this method. Pruning may be to any length fruiting canes (f.c.). Renewal spurs (r.s.) are selected so that the fruiting canes for the following year arise as near the main trunk as is practical. The 6-arm variant (Figure 9, right) is used on taller trellises. On vigorous varieties, so much foliage may have to be tied to each wire by midseason that there is a lot of shading, effective spraying is difficult, and fruit does not dry rapidly. For such vines, Umbrella Kniffin is better.

**Illustrated
Training Methods**

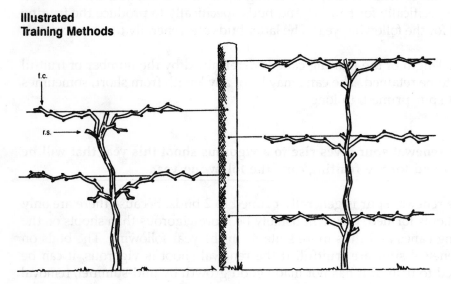

Figure 9 – Four and Six arm Kniffin.

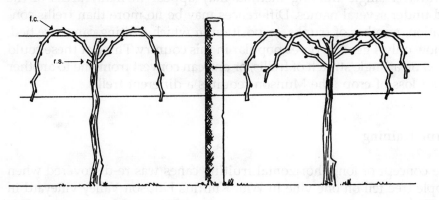

Figure 10 – Umbrella Kniffin.

Umbrella Kniffin, Figure 10, is best adapted to vigorous varieties with small or medium sized clusters that should be pruned to long canes and to varieties such as Baco noir whose buds do not break uniformly when trained horizontally. The 3 wire variant (right) can be used to adapt medium long pruning to this method. Umbrella Kniffin is not adapted to varieties that require short cane pruning. It does allow vigorous foliage to be spread out better than the Four-Arm Kniffin.

Should you think that training Riesling to the Umbrella Kniffin may cause the wine to take on a Concord-like flavor, you need only to add a couple of wires above the top of the arch and call this "halbbogenerziehung" and feel right at home in the Rheingau.

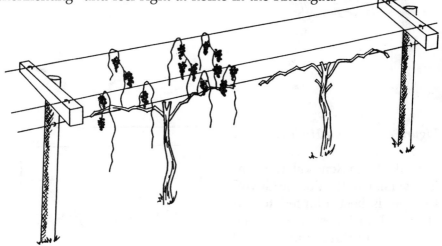

Figure 11 – Munson.

Munson (or 3-wire trough) is a modification of the Kniffin in which only 2 fruiting canes are retained and tied along the central, lower wire. New growth is draped out and over the 2 upper wires. Advantages are better fruit placement, better circulation of air for reduced disease incidence, and good exposure of foliage to light. Positioning the shoots is time consuming, trellis is more expensive, and conversion to other training methods may require development of a new main trunk. If the central wire is high enough, cross cultivation is possible through part of the season.

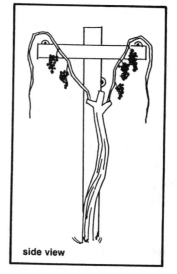

side view

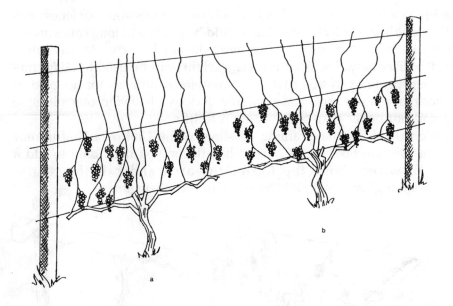

Figure 12 – Keuka High Renewal

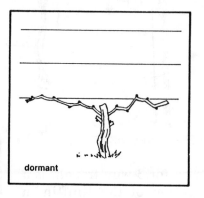

Keuka High Renewal, the American version of the double Guyot of Europe, is best adapted to large clustered varieties in which new growth is upright. Vines may be pruned (left-dormant) to any length fruiting canes required and the new shoots that bear the fruit clusters may be tied upright (a) or fanned out (b). Fruiting canes for the following year may be the 2 innermost shoots of the fruiting canes or from renewal spurs. Considerable effort is required for summer tying and varieties that produce drooping shoots are difficult to force into this configuration.

Cordon Systems of Training

The methods illustrated in this manual are all based on fruiting canes, wood of the previous season. There are several excellent training methods based on cordons — perennial, horizontal wood on which fruiting spurs of 2 to 5 buds are retained. These include the Royat of France, the Geneva Double Curtain and the single curtain methods.

With varieties or climates rarely subject to winter damage, cordon systems are often preferred. However, with many of the wine varieties grown in the eastern U.S., a cordon is subject to such frequent damage that considerable loss of crop can be expected whenever cordons must be replaced.

One should be aware of the potential value of a temporary cordon. Given a vine trained to the Keuka high renewal that fails to produce a good renewal cane, the cane that fruited the previous year can be retained, with spurs, as a cordon. Indeed, one side of a vine can be such a temporary cordon while the other is a typical renewed cane.

Arbors

The home winemaker who, in spite of a limited area available, wants to grow a few choice vines can maximize production and perhaps contribute to a pleasing landscape design through use of an arbor. There are infinite possibilities for shape, size, construction materials, and for scenic effects.

By use of the sides, as well as the top of an arbor, production can readily be doubled. If one visualizes a twelve arm Kniffin, with six arms on the sunny side of the arbor, a right angle turn and six more arms across the top of the arbor, the instructions for the Kniffin method can be adapted readily. Bud count is increased proportional to the area.

A suggested modification is to use a double trunk to reduce the time necessary to replace a damaged single trunk.

Cautions include: it is full sunlight that ripens the fruit; too high an arbor may require a ladder for pruning and harvest; and vines must be sprayed so the arbor should not be placed near picture windows, white painted walls or vegetable gardens that should not receive unwanted spray residues.

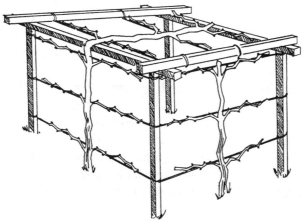

Summary Of Training Methods

The preceding sketches show textbook examples of these training methods. You will frequently have to make-do with a fruiting cane or renewal spur that arises out of optimum position. When there is a choice, plan for the future by using the buds in the best position (below wire and nearest trunk) for renewal spurs and fruit the cane in the poorer position. The shoot retained for a fruiting cane does not necessarily arise from the renewal spur of the previous season. Use the best wood available.

The "T" top form of the Munson system has proven useful in vigorous vineyards trained to other systems by serving as catch wires to spread out the leaf surfaces without summer tying.

If a vine does not respond to your guidance, allow a basal shoot to grow into a replacement trunk while retaining the old trunk and fruiting canes. Handle it as you did the young vine in Figure 2. It should form a good framework within 2 years at which time the original refractory trunk can be removed.

PRUNING

5. Pruning controls the size of the crop.

The size of the crop is determined primarily by the number of fruitful buds retained at the time of pruning. The optimum number of buds on each individual vine is determined by the vigor and productivity of that vine. Further, the number of buds should be adjusted to the cropping and unique growing conditions of the previous season. Surprisingly, this can be done by a relatively simple calculation.

6. Fruit production is competitive with vegetative growth.

A vine that is undercropped will produce a larger amount of vegetative growth than a similar vine that is overcropped. The amount of growth made by a vine during the previous season determines its potential productivity and can be measured by the weight of wood produced during that season.

This is the basis for the "balanced pruning" formulas that appear in many of the grape-growing bulletins of the eastern states. For Concord, this is a basic count of 30 buds for the first pound of *year-old* wood removed plus 10 buds for each additional pound (30 + 10) up to a maximum of 60 buds. When counting buds, those on renewal spurs are included unless a specific effort is planned to remove their fruit clusters. The formula allows anyone to prune Concord at very close to the optimum level.

Pros And Cons Of Balanced Pruning

For commercial growers with inexperienced help, balanced pruning is essential to produce maximum crops year after year. Quantity, rather than quality produces the greatest profit. The cost of labor is high, so vineyard work must be kept low.

In California, such formulas are not regularly used. In France, the laws of controlled appellation state the number of buds to be left, generally far below the optimum of a "balanced pruning". Extensive removal of vegetative growth (topping) during the growing season is done to keep vines in balance, to improve fruit quality, and promote proper wood maturity in the fall.

The amateur with a few vines will find the weighing of wood and counting of buds a useful way to begin his pruning experiences. The amateur who wishes to spend a minimum amount of time in the vineyard may wish to use an appropriate formula of balanced pruning for his vines. Table 1 can be used with most varieties once you can determine just how many clusters to remove.

TABLE 1

Balance Pruning Formulae for Mature Vines, Standard Spacings

Grape Variety	No. of buds to retain for 1st lb. of cane prunings		No. of buds added for each additional lb. of cane
Concord	30	plus	10
Fredonia	40	plus	10
Niagara	25	plus	10
Delaware, Catawba, Ives, Elvira, Dutchess	20	plus	10

French Hybrids – All of these requrie severe "sprouting and suckering" during spring and early summer for satisfactory growth, crop and vine maturity with the formulae suggested below.

Small Clustered Varieties such as Foch and Leon Millot	20	plus	10
Medium Clustered Varieties such as Aurora, Cascade, Chelios . . .	10	plus	10

In years of above average, fruit set may need cluster thinning.

Large Clustered Varieties such as Seyval, Verdelet, Villard blanc .	20	plus	10

Must supplement with pre-bloom thinning to one cluster per shoot.

Reprinted with permission of Trenholm Jordan, former Regional Extension Specialist – Grapes, Fredonia, N.Y.

Alternatives To Balanced Pruning

The amateur who is willing to devote time and thought to his pruning throughout the season can obtain several advantages in both vigor and fruit quality not available with balanced pruning.

1. Winkler points out most emphatically that removal of live wood weakens a vine. But leaving extra wood leaves extra fruit buds and the oversize crop weakens the vine for the following year. When labor for removing excess clusters is available, a marked improvement in vigor of lightly pruned vines over balanced pruning is possible. Failure to control size of the crop negates the advantage of the extra wood that is left on the vine.

2. Within limits, a smaller crop will result in higher quality wine. This is more than the simple effect of higher sugar levels. Moderate crop size results in better wine.

3. Removal of flower clusters before bloom has far less effect in reducing crop size than clusters removed after bloom. Fewer clusters at blossom time result in improved set of berries so that the clusters will be larger.

4. Cluster removal both before and after bloom will give one the option to control crop size in relation to the level of berry set. This is advantageous if rain interferes with pollination or if there is some unexpected cold-damage to flowers.

5. Unlike American and vinifera varieties, some hybrids may produce as many clusters from basal or non-count buds as from counted buds, so the crop size can not be controlled accurately by dormant pruning alone. Cluster removal is essential for these varieties.

6. As the crop size is reduced, maturity is advanced by as much as a month. This may permit late-maturing varieties to be grown in areas with shorter than optimum growing seasons. It can also lead to reduced wine quality if ripening is advanced into the hotter weather of summer.

TABLE 2

Approx. Number of Clusters Per Vine to Yield 2 to 4 Tons Per Acre

Spacing (Vines per acre)	10 x 10 (435)	9 x 9 (538)	8 x 8 (680)
Large Clusters (1 lb.).	9 – 18	7 – 15	6 – 12
Med. Clusters ($^1/_2$ lb.).	18 – 36	15 – 30	12 – 24
Small Clusters ($^1/_4$ lb.).	36 – 72	30 – 60	24 – 48

GOALS

Vines should be vigorous enough to fill the trellis, but not so vigorous as to shade adjacent vines or themselves excessively. An expression of too much shading is loss of foliage inside the canopy. About 2 pounds of wood at the time of pruning is desired.

Yields of 2 to 4 tons per acre at sugar levels of 20 to 21% sugar and acid of not over 1% with ripening as near the end of the growing season as possible are desirable for optimum wine quality. Higher yields are expected in areas where sunshine approaches 100% or when the frost-free growing season is long.

These goals can be approached on varieties adapted to your length of growing season by leaving 30 to 40 buds with a firm understanding that the crop size must be carefully controlled by cluster removal.

Table 2 indicates the number of clusters per vine to produce crops of 2 to 4 tons per acre. These are calculated for 3 spacings. Large clusters average 1 pound (as Seyval, Villard blanc, Chambourcin), medium clusters average $1/2$ pound (Vidal blanc, Chancellor, Chelois, Aurora), and small clusters average $1/4$ pound (Foch, Millot, Baco noir).

Before blossoming, remove clusters to about twice the number indicated in the table. Generally the basal cluster (nearest the trunk) is preferred because it will be the largest. This level of thinning should allow excellent set of berries. Then about 2 weeks after blossom, estimate the set of fruit. If set is good, reduce the number of clusters, retaining the biggest ones, to the number in the table.

If pollination was poor or if there was some winter-injury (all berries may fall off the tips of the clusters), cluster size will be smaller than normal and more clusters will need to be retained than given in the table. One soon develops a subjective visual appraisal of proper crop size.

This level of cluster removal should produce good results. However, other factors may upset these calculations. If these result in overcropping, symptoms are tendril abortion (June-July), lack of continued shoot growth (July-August), and if severely overcropped, poor foliage and leaf fall (July-August). When any of these symptoms appear, removal of part of the crop right up to time fruit begins to color will improve quality of the remaining fruit and reduce chances of damage from winter cold to the vines themselves.

If vines are slightly undercropped, or overly vigorous, there is nothing to do except anticipate better prospects for the following year. If, and only if, the vine is very much too vegetative, the terminal foot or so of some shoots may be removed (topping). More buds or clusters should be left the following year to balance crop and vigor. If vines continue to be overly vigorous in spite of heavier cropping, you might consider one of the training systems, such as flat-top or Geneva double curtain, to improve leaf exposure to light.

CHAPTER THREE

PLANTING AND CARE OF GRAFTED VINES

By Juergen Loenholdt

THIS CHAPTER is intended as a guide to growers planting grafted vines. Basically, the techniques employed are the same as those for own-rooted, one-year-old vines, but some procedures must be done differently and more carefully to acheive the desired results. These procedures are:

> Vine preparation
> Planting
> Care of newly planted vines
> Vineyard cultivation practices

VINE PREPARATION

Handling Grafted Vines

Healthy roots, even growth all around the base, and a complete union, are the criterions of a good grafted vine.

To check for a complete union, the so-called thumb test is used. The vine is held by the rootstock and with only the thumb, a slight pressure is applied to the scion. This test must be done delicately, because with too much force, every scion could be broken off.

Vines that do not have a proper union must be discarded. These vines would die within a few years.

Until the vines are planted, they must be stored properly to prevent the roots and graft unions from drying out. For only a few days, the vines can be kept in a cool, dark room covered with moist burlap. The vines must be checked daily, and if necessary, the roots should be watered down. For longer storage, the vines should be left at the nurseries equipped to store them.

During transportation, it is of the utmost importance that exposure to direct sunlight, wind, and dry, warm air be prevented.

Preparing The Vines Before Planting: *(Figure 1)*

Prune back the scion to one or two buds.
Remove any scion roots.
Prune back side roots close to their base.
Prune back foot roots to 4"-6" in length.

The cane must be pruned back to one or two buds. This way, only the desired one or two shoots will develop later on. It is a common mistake to cut off the old wood on the scion too close to the node. Because some tissue will dry out at every pruning cut, moisture supply to the growing shoots could be limited. Poor growth would be the result.

The old wood should be cut not closer than $1/4"$ above the node and the cut should be straight. *(Figure 2)*

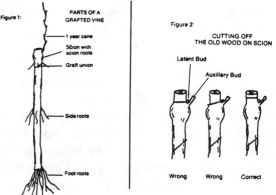

The growth of the vine is influenced by the length of the foot roots left. The length to be left must be decided by the method of planting. In no case should the roots be left too long so they bend upwards or around each other at planting. *(Figure 3)*

Pruning the vines should be done just before planting. Vines must be planted the same day they are pruned to ensure fresh, moist surface areas where the roots were cut off. From pruning to planting time, the grafted vines should be kept with their roots in water. It is a very good practice to soak the vines in water before planting, for about six hours. This allows them to regain some of the moisture which was lost during storage, and will give them a much better start.

Waxing The Vines

If the vines are not already waxed by the nursery, it is ideal to keep the bud, scion, and union from drying out by dipping the pruned vines in a paraffin specially produced for this purpose. (Available from Presque Isle

Wine Cellars, 9440 Buffalo Rd., North East, PA 16428). The paraffin is melted in a double boiler and is kept at a temperature just above its melting point, and low enough to prevent injury to the buds. The pruned vines are held upside down, dipped in cold water, then quickly dipped in the paraffin. They should be dipped deep enough so that the paraffin protects the top, down to about 2"-3" below the graft union. The paraffin will harden almost instantly. Grafted vines, protected this way, do not need to be covered over after planting, and this is the best possible way to ensure that the graft union and scion do not dry out. This protection is especially important if the vines are to be planted with the use of a grape planter. The buds have no problem growing through the paraffin.

Since grafted vines are quite an investment, this little extra effort is highly recommended. Dipping the vines in paraffin will ensure the best possible growth, and will save more time, as the vines will not have to be covered with soil after planting.

PLANTING

Like all grapevines, grafted vines must also be planted in properly-prepared soils. This fall-plowed soil should be harrowed or disced as early as possible in April, but never before it is dry enough to be worked. Marking rows and vine spacing is done in the usual way. Planting grafted vines demands special care for several reasons:

1. **The graft union must be 2" above the surface of the soil.**

2. **The graft union must be covered to keep it from drying out (if it was not waxed).**

3. **The union is the weakest part of the vine, and demands careful handling.**

(1) If planted by hand, it is easy to ensure the vines are planted at a depth which leaves the graft union 2" above the soil surface. To ensure proper planting height, place a 3' long, 2" X 2" thick piece of wood over the planting hole. Hold the graft union just above the 2" board while putting the soil back into the hole. *(Figure 4)*

Planting with a grape planter demands constant attention to keep the vines at this proper height. If the graft union is not 2" above the soil surface, the scion roots will grow, and in time (if not removed), will practically transform the vine into an own-rooted vine, thus losing the advantage of the graft.

If the graft union is left much higher than 2" above the soil surface, it

44

might dry out. Also, chances are increased that injuries from low winter temperatures will occur.

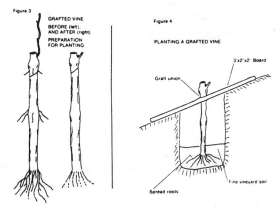

(2) Covering the graft union must be done immediately after planting. With a shovel or hoe, the fine soil should be carefully placed around the graft union to prevent it from drying out. However, the bud must be covered only very slightly or not at all. If the bud is covered too much, it will have to grow through the soil, making it very weak and often forming a crooked shoot. This additional work and its problems can be avoided if the vines are dipped in paraffin, as mentioned earlier. Waxing also ensures that the growing bud is exposed immediately to full light, and forms a very healthy shoot.

(3) Because the union is the weakest part of a grafted vine, special care must be taken not to break it off (for example, by having the compaction wheels or other parts of the planter break it off). These things demand special attention when planting grafted vines.

Fertilization

After planting, the vines can be ringed with a 10-10-10, 10-5-20, or similar fertilizer. Use about $^1/_4$ lb. per vine and spread about 3″ to 6″ around the vines (not directly on top of the plant). This will ensure a good start for the vines, and must be applied soon after planting.

CARE OF THE PLANTED VINES

Immediately after planting, the soil in the aisles should be loosened by cultivation. If at all possible, the post should be placed, and at least one wire attached to have support available for the new growing shoot. It is ideal to place at each vine, a small stick (6′ wood lath or something similar), to which the young shoot can be tied at regular intervals. If this is done, only one shoot has to be left. Since it can grow upright, it is stimulated to grow faster and will form a good, straight trunk the first year. If left on the ground, laterals are formed in large numbers and the resulting "bush" must be pruned back to near-ground level the second year. This can also be prevented by placing a string from the vine to the lowest trellis wire and tying the shoot regularly to this string until it reaches the wire.

Bud Break

As soon as the buds on the newly-planted vines start growing, all little shoots except one (two if no support is available) must be removed. Not the biggest, but the one best-located shoot should be left. This usually is the one forming from the latent bud *(Figure 2)*, because this one will form the vertical extension of the scion and the best-possible, straight, and healthy trunk.

Tying this developing shoot at regular intervals (about every 5 to 7 inches), and removing the laterals, has a definite influence on the development of the trunk. Bast or plastic tying material is preferred because it will prevent girdling. If laterals are left, they will prevent the main growing tip from growing as much as possible. The laterals must be removed at the beginning of their development, before they form leaves. If left too long, their removal will leave wounds on the shoot, which can result later in the trunk dying back or growing weak. After the shoot reaches the height desired for a trunk, the laterals do not have to be removed above that height. A trunk developed this way during its first growing season, is completely free from pruning wounds, and thus will withstand low winter temperatures much better.

Insect And Disease Control

The newly planted vines must be checked frequently to guard against insect and disease damage. Many grape growers are still under the impression that spraying young vines is not needed. Nothing is further from the truth. For example, young vines have very few leaves, so if some or all are infected by mildew, or damaged by insects, development of the vines will be slowed. Powdery mildew infection (and the resulting reduced foliage) delays wood maturity leaving the vines less winter hardy.

Depending on grape variety, young vines must be sprayed at least as often as mature vineyards. If frequent, close examinations show signs of insect or mildew infection, more sprays are needed.

Vines must be kept completely healthy until late fall when the foliage is killed by the first frost. **Contact your local County Agricultural Extension Agent and follow the spray program recommended for your area.** For example, good control can be accomplished in Western New York by using:

Captan 50 WP — 2 lbs per 100 gallons water

Sulfur* — 2 lbs per 100 gallons water

Seven 50 WP — 2 lbs per 100 gallons water

On sulfur susceptible varieties replace the sulfur with:

Benmyl 50 WP- 1/2 lb per 100 gallons water

Adjust sprayer nozzles to get good coverage on the young vines' growth.

*Use sulfur only on sulfur-tolerant varieties for control of powdery mildew. On varieties susceptible to sulfur use: Benomyl 50 WP — $^1/_2$ lb. per 100 gals. water.

CULTIVATION

In a young vineyard, the soil should always be kept open to provide better growing conditions than compacted, closed soils. Weed growth must be prevented, because weeds grow faster than the vines and take away light, air and water.

To protect the graft union from winter injury, the vines must be hilled up in late fall. This is absolutely necessary. Many vines will be lost if this is neglected. With a suitable plow, a good mound must be formed to cover the graft union with at least 6"-8" of soil. Care must be taken not to leave a deep, open furrow near the vines. An open furrow could lead to winter injury to the roots, and also increases erosion.

Following the plow with a disc is one efficient way to close the furrows after hilling the vines. A cultivator or drag also performs well.

The following year, late in April or in May, the mound must be carefully plowed away and the ridge left between the vines must be removed by a mechanical grape hoe. To avoid damage to the vines, care must be taken to ensure the take-out is not operated too close to the vines. Immediately after, the soil directly around the vines should be hoed away by hand. At this time, any scion roots which have developed, must be cut off. Following the removal of the ridge of soil and the hand hoeing, weeds should be prevented from growing between the vines during the period that the young vines are making their greatest growth. Regular rates of vineyard herbicides can be used to control weeds underneath the trellis after the first three growing seasons.

The removal of the soil mound from the graft union is a must, to prevent the growth of scion roots.

During the second growing season, regular cultivation between the rows will prevent weed growth and stimulate vine growth. Missing vines must be replanted during the spring of the second year.

Pruning And Trunk Development

The growth of only one shoot the first year, makes possible a perfect trunk the second year. The length of the trunk left for the second year depends on its growth during the first year, the length desired, the type of rootstock, and the fertility of the soil. The following table can be used as a rough guide.

	No. of buds to be left in second year	
Length of one-year cane	Poor Soil	Good Soil
Less than 4″	Replant	Replant
4″ to 6″	Prune back to 2	2
6″ to 12″	2	3
12″ to 24″	3	4
24″ to 35″	4	5
35″ to 46″	5	6
46″ to 60″	6	7
Over 60″	6	8

Which buds should you leave? Since the cane is never matured to its full length, it must be pruned back from the top until the wood is green. Below that point, the buds are healthy, and the desired number of buds are left from here down. If the green, healthy cane is longer than the desired trunk height, two buds should be left below the desired trunk height. The number of buds desired will determine the length of the cane to be cut off. Leaving two buds below the desired trunk height will make sure that the head is at the proper height the following year.

Pruning back to only two buds near ground level must be done only if the first year's shoot grew less than 6″ high. Vines that grew less than 4″ on a single shoot must be replanted with a new grafted vine. Their poor growth is almost always a sign that the rootstock was deficient or that the graft union was not properly joined. The greatest advantage of training only one shoot during the first growing season is that it usually develops a strong cane with short nodes. The trunk from such a cane is much more frost-hardy.

If, during the first year, more than one shoot was left, the trunk should be developed from the lowest one with the least number of wounds.

Debudding

The removal of all buds below those desired is very important. It should be done very early, after bud break, and before the first leaves can develop on them. At this early stage, they are very easily stripped off by hand and will not leave wounds. If buds are removed by pruning shears, or removed after leaves were formed on them, large wounds will result. The tissue at the wounds will dry out and the trunk will often grow only on one side. These trunks age fast and must be renewed soon.

Pruning should be done before bud break, so that the young vines do not bleed excessively. To develop a straight trunk, vines must be carefully tied. Willows or plastic tying materials are ideal, because they prevent girdling. If wire twist ties or string is used, the vines must be tied very loosely to prevent girdling.

Replanting During The Second Year

All missing or poor vines should be replanted the second year. This must not be overlooked, because during the third growing season, the normally-developed vines will shade the replants so much that they develop poorly. Also, it is all too common to neglect these replants, and not give them the proper care they demand. Spraying and cultivation should be done as during the first year.

Hilling The Graft Union

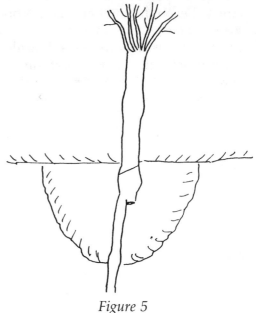

To cover the graft union with soil for frost protection can be done the second year, in late July or early August. The trunk should then be sturdy enough so that it is not damaged by the soil. It must be ensured that after the soil has settled, the graft union is still covered with 4" to 6" of soil, and thus protected. After hilling and filling in the plow furrows, it is advisable to seed a cover crop between the rows. This will prevent erosion and also help vine maturity. Oats is a good cover crop, because (unlike

Figure 5

rye) it will not grow in the spring, making it more difficult to plow the soil away from the vines. This, and taking out under the vines, must be done the same as during the second season.

Pruning during the third season must be done according to growth. In most cases, two short canes can be left, with six to ten buds on each. Depending on vine development, one cluster per shoot should be left, to get a small crop the third year. It is important, not to get more fruit, because this will weaken the vine enough to set it back seriously.

Training and fertilization the third season should be done the same way as recommended for own-rooted vines of the same variety. Also, the usual disease and insect control is recommended.

Soil cultivation is the same as during the second growing season.

The only major difference from growing own-rooted vines, is that the graft union must be covered by soil to protect it from winter injury, and must be uncovered in the spring to prevent the development of scion roots. If this is done carefully for the first three to five years, very few scion roots will develop. After careful observation, and depending on conditions, it might be possible to leave the graft union covered with soil and use normal herbicide sprays to keep the mound under the vines free from weeds. However, the vines should be checked periodically during the growing season. As soon as developing scion roots are observed, they must be removed.

As with all young vineyards, the sucess or failure will depend directly on the proper care and attention the vineyard receives. It can not be stressed enough how important proper care during the first few years is for deciding if the vineyard will ever be a profitable operation. Unfortunately, too many growers still neglect the care of their young vineyards. Then they blame the poor performance of their vines on all other possible explanations, rather than putting the blame where it belongs.

A vineyard planting is too great an investment to neglect it!

CHAPTER FOUR

THE GRAPE VINE AS AN INVESTMENT

By John R. McGrew, PhD.

IN THIS CHAPTER I shall offer an analogy between a grapevine and a business enterprise. An understanding of the economic interrelationships among the various parts of the vine will show how damage to a part of the vine can affect the operation or even survival of the rest of the vine.

The basic operation of a vine is the conversion of light energy to sugar. Light received by green leaves, plus carbon dioxide from the air plus water and minerals from the soil are the raw materials of sugar fabrication.

Part of these sugars are required by living cells throughout the vine to maintain life processes. This consumption is analogous to operating costs. Another portion of the sugar is utilized to develop new growth of stems, leaves and roots. This we shall call capital improvements. Because the vine ceases normal operations during winter dormancy, an internal source of energy is required to re-establish growth in the spring. This source is from sugars stored as starch in the stems and roots and this requirement is analogous to reserve funds.

Sugars in excess of those required for operating costs, capital improvements and reserve funds are available in the form of fruit and represent profits paid as dividends to the investor.

There are many maladies which affect one or more parts of the vine. Representative samples will show the overall effect of various forms of damage.

Leaves

A mature vine requires from six (Tokay variety in California) to eight (Concord variety in New York) square feet of leaf area to produce a profit of one pound of fruit. Physical loss of leaf area can result from such agents as insects, fungus diseases, grazing by animals, or herbicide damage. Reduction in the effectiveness of leaf area results from shading, mineral deficiencies or toxicities, herbicide damage, and many other factors.

The overall effect is a reduction in sugar production which can result in a smaller crop, reduced fruit quality, or a weakened vine.

Stems

The trunk, canes, and shoots serve as support for leaves and fruit to transport sugars from the leaves and to transport water and minerals from the roots to leaves and areas of new growth.

Interference with these functions result from such situations as girdling, crown gall, dead arm fungus disease, failure of sufficient fruiting wood to mature before frost, and traumatic damage from cultivation equipment.

Severe damage results in the loss of the crop but, if the base of the vine and root system are not damaged, the vine can resprout from stored reserves.

Fruit

Sugars accumulate in large quantities in the fruit during the final month or so of fruit development. If the flowers or young fruit are removed, as by spring frost, black rot or other fungus diseases, or by overpruning, the vine will return to an unnecessary and unproductive vigorous capital improvement situation.

If the fruit is removed after sugar accumulation, as by birds, fruit rots, late berry moth, etc., the effect on the vine will not differ from normal harvest. The only potential lethal effect of repeated fruit removal is the discouragement of the grower to the point that he pulls out the vineyard.

Roots

The root system must provide the vine each year on an acre basis with 20 to 50 inches of water and 20 to 70 pounds of nitrogen, 20 to 50 pounds of potash, and 3 to 6 pounds of phosphoric oxide. In addition, small quantities of about a dozen trace elements are required for proper growth.

If water or any of the minerals are not available, obviously the vine will be adversely affected. If there is too much water for an extended period, the roots will be damaged. Excessive fertilizer on young vines, saline soils, or toxic levels of minor elements can be equally damaging to roots.

Root-rotting fungi are seldom a major problem. Cotton root rot in the black alkaline soils of the South Central States and Armillaria root rot do affect grapes, but these are troubles which affect a wide range of host plants and will be recognized on other host plants in the area.

Two insects are serious and specific parasites of the grape. Phylloxera attacks all vinifera grapes and some of the French hybrids. This pest is especially destructive on heavy soils. There is a renewed appreciation of the damage from the grapevine root-borer throughout the Southeastern States, from Missouri to Georgia, and north to West Virginia and Maryland.

Nematodes, root-knot and root-lesion, are sometimes severe, especially on old vineyard sites.

Rootstocks can be selected to reduce the damage from most of these soil conditions or pests. Some root-stock varieties are adapted to dry soils, high lime, and to various levels of soil fertility. Some have resistance to nematodes, to phylloxera, or to both.

If the root system of a vine is damaged or if it fails to perform its necessary functions, the vine is weakened and will eventually succumb.

Overcropping

We now come to the situation in the operation of a grapevine which results, I believe, in more dead vines than all the types of maladies we have mentioned.

Fruit takes precedence over all other demands for sugar in the growth of a vine. As the size of the crop is increased, the amount of sugar available for maintenance, capital improvements and reserves is decreased. Not only are these vital operations reduced, but with an oversized crop there is not enough sugar to develop good fruit quality. Sugar content is low, acid high, color poor and maturity is delayed.

There are entirely too many factors to permit one to predict the proper crop size. Under French regulations, the permitted harvest varies from $1/2$ ton to 14 tons per acre depending on variety. Within a variety, the permitted yield may vary over a 3-fold difference depending on location of the vineyard.

If we know what to look for, the vine will give us a pretty good indication of the status of its internal supply and demand of sugar.

As the demand for sugar exceeds the available supply, the first sign will be the failure of tendrils to develop on some of the new shoots. If all the new growth has a full complement of tendrils through July and August, the crop is smaller than optimum.

As the crop size is increased, the new shoots will stop growing. You will find few, if any, new leaves being formed, and a look at the ends of the shoots will show that the small leaves present are mature and not young and tender.

If there is a severe overcropping, the sugar required for maintenance of the leaves is diverted to the fruit. Leaves scald and drop, thus cutting off any further production of sugar. Reserves are depleted just when they are needed most to carry the vine through the winter.

Thus, on a vine carrying an optimum crop, considering both quantity and quality of the fruit, a few of the shoots should continue to grow right through the ripening phase. Severity of pruning, determines the size of the crop and if the grower has underpruned, clusters can be removed right up to the time of sugar accumulation to allow the vine enough sugar to carry out its necessary operations.

In summary, keep the vines in a capital improvement program until they reach optimum size whether this takes two years or four years. Then declare yourself a reasonable dividend and have a happy vintage.

CHAPTER FIVE

FOLIAR NUTRITION

By Thomas J. Zabadal, PhD.

T HE MERITS of foliar nutrition of grapevines are often pondered by many grpae growers. Sometimes growers observe abnormal vine growth and wonder if a foliar spray might be helpful. More often there is no apparent limitation or abnormality of vine growth, but nevertheless, a grower wonders if foliar nutrition just might improve vineyard productivity. I believe this attitude is much like the use of daily multiple vitamins by many people. That is, we don't know that we are deficient in vitamins or minerals in our diet. However, we ponder that perhaps we have nutritional deficiencies in our diet and vitamin pills might help! At worst we are just wasting vitamin pills.

Similarly, growers sometimes look at foliar nutrition as possibly doing good but at worst doing no harm. Our intent is to review foliar nutrition in regard to grapevines.

Nutrients Limiting Grapevine Growth

There are 16 nutrients known to be essential for the growth of plants. However, for grapevines in eastern U.S. vineyards, only 6 of these nutrients have ever been shown to limit vine growth. Three of these are macronutrients, that is, they are generally required in parts per hundereds in the dry weight of the plant material. These are nitrogen, potassium and magnesium. The other three nutrients that can be limiting are called micronutrients bacause they are found only in parts per million in plant tissues. These are manganese, iron and boron. To my knowledge no other nutrients have been documented as being in short supply in eastern U.S. vineyards.

Plant Response To Foliar Nutrition

The scientific literature on foliar nutrition is extensive, and it well documents that plants can respond significantly to foliar nutrition. Therefore, in principle this approach to nutrition is worthy of consideration. However, the indiscriminate application of foliar sprays to grapevines is unjustified. First of all, the potential for benefit is limited to the 6 nutrients just mentioned. Secondly, the application of some of these nutrients is questionable.

Nitrogen

Grapevines can exhibit a quick response to foliar nitrogen applications. Pale yellow-green, nitrogen deficient leaves can show an increase in green coloration in a few days time when foliar sprays are applied. However, the scientific literature indicates a variable cropping response to foliar nitrogen sprays. Some studies on apples indicate a significant crop response to multiple nitrogen foliar sprays. However, a study of Concord grapes revealed that no benefit was obtained on vines, which were already receiving soil applications of nitrogen fertilizers. It is likely that foliar sprays could alleviate nitrogen deficiencies in grapevines caused by inadequate soil fertilization applications, but they will not improve vineyards which are receiving adequate soil nitrogen applications and exhibit good green leaf color.

When making foliar nitrogen applications, the material of choice is urea at the rate of 5 lbs. per 100 gallons of water. Some fertilizer grades of urea may contain a contaminant called biuret, which can cause leaf burn. Therefore, growers ought to purchase "feed grade" urea for foliar spraying. This material may be applied in combination with most commonly used pesticides.

Magnesium

Eastern U.S. vineyards exhibit signs of magnesium deficiency with some frequency due to low soil pH and low magnesium supply, or excess potash fertilization. Vines respond well to foliar magnesium sprays. The typical material used is magnesium sulfate (Epsom salts) at a rate of 10 lbs. per acre in 40 to 100 gallons of water. Applications should be made in the first two postbloom sprays in combination with most commonly used pesticides. Compatibility with emulsifiable concentrates is unknown.

Potassium

Research indicates that grapevine leaves will absorb potassium sprays. However, research on several other crops indicates that when plants are provided adequate potassium through soil fertilizer applications, it is unlikely that foliar potassium sprays will result in an increased crop response. Solutions of 1% potassium sulfate have been used. However, these sprays have occasionally resulted in leaf injury. Petiole tests provide the most reliable method of assuring adequate potash levels in vineyards and avoiding the appearance of potash deficiency symptoms in vines. However, if such a program is not followed, and a grower observes potash deficiency symptoms in his vineyard, he ought to consider immediate soil applications of potash fertilizers rather than attempting to remedy the matter with one or more foliar sprays.

Boron

Grapevines can exhibit an increased crop response to foliar boron sprays. However, because boron is a micronutrient, phytotoxicity of grapevine leaves is very possible with excess applications. Therefore, boron foliar sprays ought to be applied only when prior petiole tests indicate such a need. Moreover, it is important to realize that the principle benefit of boron foliar sprays is an increase in berry set. Therefore, in vineyards where the set of berries is considered adequate or excessive, boron sprays are unjustified.

Where boron sprays are warranted, two sprays should be applied, one about 10 days before the start of bloom and the other at the start of bloom. There is no benefit from post-bloom foliar boron sprays. For each of these sprays a maximum rate of $1/2$ pound of actual boron per acre, or $2^1/2$ pounds of Solubor is suggested. However, several applications in Finger Lakes vineyards at that rate have resulted in injury to grapevine foliage. Therefore, a grower ought to apply at this rate on a trial basis only. A rate that has been safely and effectively used on apple trees has been 0.2 lbs. of actual boron or 1.0 lbs. of Solubor per acre in 100 gallons of water.

Manganese

Deficiency symptoms of this element can be found occasionally, however, the extent of this deficiency seldom warrants corrective measures. Nevertheless, there are situations when it is justified to eliminate a manganese deficiency. Various materials have been used including manganese chelate sprays. Manganese sulfate sprays at a rate of 2-5 lbs. per 100 gallons of water per acre have also been used. It has been observed that the use of maneb fungicides can result in a greening of grapevine leaves, presumably the result of manganese foliar fertilization.

In summary, it is possible to foliar fertilize grapevines with manganese.

However, there will be relatively few situations in which such activity would result in a measurable crop response.

Iron

Iron deficiency is typically found on alkaline soils. The Diamond and Catawba varieties appear to be most affected. There is extensive scientific literature relating to the treatment of iron deficiency in many crops. With very few exceptions, treatments to alleviate iron deficiency have not provided an economic benefit. It is possible to reduce iron chlorosis of grapevine leaves with iron chelate or ferrous sulfate (5 lbs. per 100 gallons of water) foliar sprays. The use of the fungicide ferbam has also been recommended to reduce iron chlorosis. However, none of these foliar treatments has, in my experience, resulted in an increase in vine vigor and crop level. Moreover, extensive trials of soil amendments to alleviate iron deficiency have not provided commercially useful results.

In summary, 6 nutrients can be identified, which are sometimes deficient in grapevines growing in eastern U.S. vineyards. Under certain conditions foliar applications of 4 of these nutrients may be considered. These 4 include 2 macronutrients, nitrogen and magnesium, and 2 micronutrients, boron and manganese.

On the other hand, there would seem to be little justification for foliar applications of potassium or iron. Potassium deficiencies should be handled by soil fertilizer applications.

For nutrients other than the 6 mentioned above, there is no justification, based on current scientific literature, for their application in eastern U.S. vineyards. Therefore, before a grower purchases any foliar fertilizer, he ought to be certain that there is a justification for its use.

CHAPTER SIX

A REVIEW OF THE ORIGIN OF INTERSPECIFIC HYBRID GRAPE VARIETIES

By John R. McGrew, PhD.

THE CULTIVATED varieties of grapes that embody the highest qualities for table, raisin, and wine use are derived entirely from the genetic complement of the single, old world species, *Vitis vinifera*. In spite of this, about $1/5$ of the grapes cultivated around the world are interspecific hybrids between *V. vinifera* and wild species of *Vitis*. This chapter will attempt to answer three questions:

1. Which wild species have been used?

2. Why were they used?

3. When and where were the interspecific hybrids originated?

The Species

The botanical classifications of grapes include, depending on whose monograph is used, about 60 species. These are divided into two groups, the larger being *Euvitis*, or true grapes, and the *Muscadinia*, including the muscadines as represented by Scuppernong.

About half the *Euvitis* species are native to North America and about a dozen of these have been profitably incorporated into interspecific hybrids. *V. vinifera* is native to Asia, Asia Minor and Europe. The balance are Asian and range from tropical to cold climate adaptation. Within *Euvitis*, the species are generally interfertile and hybridization is successful.

Extensive descriptions of all the known species of *Vitis* appear in various botanical publications, but here I shall give brief descriptions of only those species which have been used in interesting or useful hybrids. Omitted are several species which were tried in France without success and a group of species native to Florida which have been utilized in a relatively successful program to develop Pierce's Disease resistant table grapes.

V. rupestris – Sand grape. Small berries, small to medium clusters, wild taste, vigorous, roots easily, pest resistant.

V. Lincecumii – Post oak grape. Medium to large berries, small to medium clusters, distinctive wild taste in no way resembling that of the fox grapes, fair pest resistance.

V. aestivalis – Summer grape. (Included in this is *V. Bourquiniana* — southern summer grape.) Small to medium berries, medium to large, open clusters, high sugar and acid, fair pest resistance.

V. labrusca – Fox grape. Large berries, small clusters, distinctive and strong flavor, fair pest resistance.

V. Berlandieri – Spanish grape. Berries small, clusters medium, adapted to lime soils, moderate pest resistance.

V. riparia (sometimes = *V. vulpina*) – Riverbank grape. Small berries and clusters, wide variation in ripening and hardiness, vigorous, roots easily, fair to good pest resistance.

V. Longii (= *V. Solonis*) – Bush or Panhandle grape. Medium berries, small clusters, early ripening. Roots easily and adapted to moderately limy soils. Used mainly in rootstock breeding.

V. Champini – Relatively rare species native to Texas. Small clusters of medium sized berries. Vigorous, roots easily, adapted to lime soils, resistant to nematodes and other pests, primarily rootstock.

V. cordifolia – Winter or Frost grape. Small berries, medium size open clusters. Late ripening, bitingly pungent until well after frost, even then with a strong wild taste. Very vigorous, native over a wide area. Pest resistance medium to poor.

V. monticola – Sweet Mountain grape. Another Texas species, small clusters of medium berries. Moderate vigor, poor rooting, adapted to dry and limy soils.

V. candicans – Mustang grape. Small clusters of medium to large berries with tough skin and a biting pungency. Apparently tolerant of Pierce's disease as well as other pests and used in desperation only where no other grapes survive.

V. rotundifolia and *V. Munsoniana* are *Muscadinia* species, with a different chromosome number from the *Euvitis*. Because of this difference, the hybrids with *Euvitis* are usually unfruitful. Fruitful hybrid lines are possible and have potential value. These species have large berry size, small clusters, and mild to strong, distinctive flavors. They root poorly, are more cold tender than *V. vinifera*, but have excellent tolerance to several diseases and insects.

A single Asiatic species of *Euvitis, V. amurensis* is being used to a limited extent by some European breeders for its hardiness to low winter temperatures. The appalling flavor of this species requires repeated backcrossing to vinifera before useful cultivars are obtained.

Pests Of The Vine

There are four major pests of the vine native to North America. Three of these, powdery mildew, downy mildew and black rot are fungus diseases affecting foliage and fruit. The fourth is an insect, the grape phylloxera, which may produce obvious leaf galls, but whose major damage is destruction of the roots. The North American species evolved, by necessity, with a tolerance to these pests. The Asian and vinifera grapes, which evolved in the absence of these pests, are very susceptible and may be severely damaged.

The best of the wild grapes of North America are much inferior to the cultivated viniferas of Europe, so there has been a continuous importation of viniferas from the earliest Colonial times. The combination of pests and perhaps the more variable climate caused the viniferas to fail rapidly. Their culture was unprofitable in all but such favored locations as Mexico and California.

Origin Of American Varieties

The grape growers of the East made do with what was available after the failure of the viniferas. At first, they collected the fruit of the native vines, or transplanted these to vineyards where they optimistically hoped, by cultivation, to improve the wine quality.

Examples of American varieties entirely free of vinifera admixture are rare today. It is possible that Franklin contains only *V. labrusca* and *V. riparia* and that Munson (Jaeger 70) is pure *V. rupestris* by pure *V. Lincecumii.*

The major portion of American varieties do carry along with their inheritance from North American species both the improved fruit quality and perfect flowers derived from *V. vinifera*. The American varieties appeared at first by chance and then by design. Their value rests on the combination of pest resistance from the American species with the fruit qualities of *V. vinifera.*

Into these and another nearly 2000 varieties named before 1900, there was incorporated an almost unlimited range of pest resistant species material with a narrow choice of vinifera parentage.

The American varieties are often lumped together under such terms as labrusca or *V. labruscana* . This is not entirely fair because a portion of these are derived from species other than *V. labrusca.* The parentages of the older American varieties are not known, but we can recognize to a fair degree which species were involved.

The speciation of many American varieties appears in the "Grapes of New York" and in a 1938 report of the varieties growing in the USDA vineyard at Arlington Farms. From these sources, Table 1 shows the percentage of the 225 selected varieties in which each of 7 native species and *V. vinifera* are present.

Of the 17 varieties in which *V. labrusca* is not present, several are the southern *V. aestivalis* varieties such as Lenoir and Herbemont. More than half are Munson varieties derived from *V. Lincecumii* rather than from *V. labrusca*. As a group, these varieties represent the more successful combinations of adaptation to climate, pest tolerance and fruit (if not wine) quality.

TABLE 1

Species present in 225 American varieties of grapes

	Percent		Percent
V. vinifera	68	V. Lincecumii	14
V. labrusca	92	V. rupestris	7
V. aestivalis	30	V. Champinii	2
V. riparia	16	V. candicans	0.4

American Pests Come To France

In France, centuries of experience has resulted in selection of only the choicest viniferas for each geographical and climatic area. Into this completely susceptible population of grapes the phylloxera was introduced about 1860. The spread of this insect destroyed about 90% of French vineyards in the following 20 years.

The first successful countermeasure, and a temporary one it turned out, was the planting of American varieties. There were over 25,000 acres of Noah in France at one time. Clinton, Othello, Lenoir (Jacquez), Isabella and Herbemont were leading varieties. Concord, Catawba, and Delaware were tried, but rejected for their low resistance to phylloxera rather than taste.

With the flood of planting stock from America came both downy mildew and black rot to further plague the French vineyardist.

The ultimate control of the American pests was two-fold. By 1876 it was shown that by grafting onto American types, the viniferas could be protected against phylloxera. In 1885 the first broad spectrum fungicide, Bordeaux mixture, was discovered and used successfully to protect leaves and fruit from the fungus diseases. The combination permitted France to return to a position of world leadership in wine production from pure viniferas.

Origin Of The Rootstock Varieties

Between 1875 and 1900, viticultural institutions and amateur breeders in Europe developed some 1500 different rootstock varieties which involved many combinations of American species. Sometimes *V. vinifera*, even though susceptible to phylloxera, was used to improve compatibility of grafts and rootability of the rootstock. The breeding of new rootstocks is still under way, yet from all these combinations, only about 40 rootstock varieties are presently in use in Europe and California. These 40 provide the required adaptation for resistance to phylloxera and/or nematodes, various soil types and levels of vigor.

The origins of these rootstocks are relatively simple and well documented, so we can determine which species were used and the level of contribution of each species. These are shown in Table 2.

TABLE 2

Species in, and level of contribution when present for 40 rootstock varieties.

Species	Present in Percent	Level of Contribution Avg. Percent	(Range)
V. riparia	65	45	(00-100)
V. rupestris	45	50	(25-100)
V. Berlandieri	42.5	50	(50)
V. vinifera	27.5	35	(15-50)
V. Longii	15	29	(25-50)
V. labrusca	10	9.4	(3-25)
V. Champinii	10	75	(50-100)
V. cordifolia	7.5	33	(25-50)
V. monticola	2.5	50	

Five rootstocks of three species were suitable, without hybridization. *V. Chaminii* is used only in California, primarily for its tolerance to nematodes in sandy soils. *V. Berlandieri* is useful in France because of its tolerance to lime soils.

The demonstrated value of these 40 rootstock varieties is based on performance of individual vine varieties, each with its unique genetic combination. From among thousands of *V. Berlandieri* x *V. riparia* seedlings, Sigmund Teleki of Hungary selected only three that are in present use. Other breeders have selected an additional six hybrids of this same species combination. From this table, we can see which species have given rise to successful rootstocks, but not how many thousands of failures resulted from similar hybrids or combinations with other species.

Origin Of The French Hybrids

A few of the thousands of hybrids developed primarily for rootstocks bore fruit which was equal in quality to the American varieties then being grown in France. It was the amateur grape breeders of France who pursued the goal of hybrid direct producers, vines with roots resistant to phylloxera, foliage resistant to fungus diseases and fruit that would produce wines more like viniferas than the available American varieties. The amateur breeders who were most active between 1885 and 1930 grew hundreds of thousands of seedlings of which perhaps 3000 have been tried commercially.

These hybrid direct producers, known in the U.S. as French hybrids and in Europe as American hybrids, are referred to by the name or initials of the hybridizer plus his selection number. A few have received names, some from the hybridist, some officcially from the French Ministry of Agriculture, and some from the Finger Lakes Wine Growers Association in Naples, New York.

The first stage, or ancient, hybrids were the crosses of American varieties, or rootstock varieties with vinifera. Examples of this stage are Baco noir which is Folle blanche (vinifera) by a wild *V. riparia* and Baco blanc which is Folle blanche by Noah, an American variety derived from *V. labrusca, V. riparia* and *V. vinifera.* The hybrids of Ganzin, Kuhlmann, Couderc and the early Seibels are also of this stage.

The vinifera varieties used successfully in the first stage hybrids were those with large clusters or berries, as Aramon, Clairette and Cinsaut. The premium wine varieties were tried repeatedly, but none of the resulting hybrids were acceptable.

The sources of resistance used were sometimes American varieties derived from *V. labrusca,* but extensive use was also made of *V. Bourquinia* (as Lenoir) and of Jaeger 70, a cross between *V. Lincecumii* and *V. rupestris.*

The second stage hybrids are the crosses between hybrids. This type of hybridization often extended for several generations and has led to some complex genealogies. Most of the Seibel, Bertille Seyve, Joanes Seyve, Seyve Villard, Galibert and Landot hybrids are of this group.

This interbreeding of hybrid by hybrid allowed for little or no return to sources of resistance from the wild species or to sources of improved fruit quality from superior viniferas. There has been an extensive reshuffling of genetic characters which allowed selection of improved types for certain areas, soils or uses.

The third stage, sometimes referred to as the modern hybrids, involved crosses of hybrids with viniferas of superior wine quality. For example: Ravat 6 is Seibel 8724 by Chardonnay, Ravat 262 is S 8365 by Pinot noir, Ravat 51 is S 6905 by Pinot blanc and Vidal 256 is Ugni blanc by S 4986.

In this third stage, there is unfortunately a progressive dilution of resistance. Even when Ravat 6 was the most widely "recommended" hybrid for A.O.C. in France, there were less than 1000 acres grown. In France, Ravat 6 must be grafted, requires three sprays for control of downy mildew and two to three sulfur sprays for control of powdery mildew, and offered little advantage over available vinifera varieties.

The parentages of many of the hybrid direct producers have been reported in the French literature. There are questions regarding accuracy and some differences of opinion. I am grateful to Pierre Galet for checking a set of genealogies and for accepting some of my own guesses on the derivation of American varieties that are involved.

These genealogies go back as much as 8 generations of interspecific hybridization and many include as many as 7 different species in a single hybrid. An analysis of the species derivation and degree of contribution of each species could be made for several hundred hybrids. I have selected 50 on the basis of their superior performance: 24 from the "recommended" or "authorized" list of 1964 by the French IVCC, 25 from recent Boordy Vineyard and New York State Fruit Testing Cooperative Association catalogs, plus Cayuga White. At least another dozen hybrids on these lists were omitted because parentages are not known.

If all the hybrids of known parentage were included in such an analysis, the positive contribution of each species would be lost among the many varieties that have been tried and discarded by growers or winemakers.

In order to demonstrate the presence and contribution of species to a variety, one of the simpler genealogies is shown in Figure 1.

In Seibel 4986 (Rayon d'Or) we find only three species present: *V. vinifera*, *V. rupestris* and *V. Lincecumii*. However, *V. vinifera* is found as one grandparent ($^4/_{16}$) and as two great-grandparents ($^2/_{16}$ and $^2/_{16}$). The total contribution of this species is $^8/_{16}$ or 50%. *V. rupestris* appears three times and contributes $2/16 + 2/16 + 1/16$ or 31.25%. Finally, *V. Lincecumii* contributes $2/16 + 1/16$ or 18.75%.

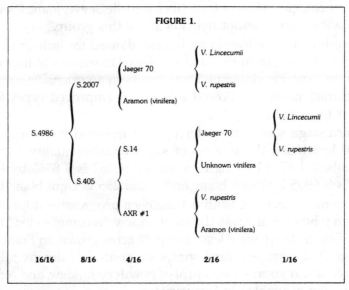

FIGURE 1.

Figure 1.

The contribution depends both on how often and at which generation each species is involved. The calculations can be complex. Of the 31 hybrids in which *V. labrusca* was present, this species appeared at 16 different levels of contribution.

Data were obtained for 9 first, 33 second and 8 third stage hybrids. These stages can be considered steps in the development towards higher quality varieties.

TABLE 3

Species present by percent, in 50 hybrid direct producers.

	STAGE			
	First	Second	Third	TOTAL
	(9)	(33)	(8)	(50)
V. vinifera	100	100	100	100
V. rupestris	67	97	100	92
V. Lincecumii	22	97	100	84
V. aestivalis[1]	0	82	50	62
V. labrusca	11	73	37.5	56
V. Berlandieri	0	42	25	32
V. riparia	44	33	0	26

[1]Includes *V. Bourguiniana*.

The species present at each stage (Table 3) show marked changes. The valuable contributions of *V. Lincecumii* (from Jaeger 70) were quickly recognized and used extensively. On the other hand, *V. riparia* gives hybrids of good appearance but moderate quality and was completely eliminated from the third stage hybrids.

The presence of *V. labrusca* in most of the American varieties available to the earlier hybridists resulted in many first stage hybrids with major labrusca inheritance. Of these, only 1 (Baco blanc) was of sufficient quality to appear on this list. But many first stage labrusca hybrids entered into the second stage hybrids and some labrusca inheritances are present in almost $3/4$ of them. Third stage hybrids show a discrimination against the presence of *V. labrusca* and its pervasive flavors in the search for higher quality.

Data on the contribution of the several species appear in Table 4. These percentages are based only on those hybrids in which each species appears,(the number of hybrids in each group can be calculated from Table 3) so each column totals more than 100%.

TABLE 4

Average contribution and range ( ) by percent of each species, when present, in 50 hybrid direct producers.

	First (9)		Second (33)		Third (8)		TOTAL (50)	
V. vinifera	55	(50-69)	53	(42-82)	78	(72-83)	61	(42-83)
V. rupestris	29	(25-50)	25	(12-41)	13	(7-19)	23	(7-50)
V. Lincecumii	25	(25)	8	(3-19)	5	(3-9)	8.5	(3-25)
V. aestivalis[1]	—		5	(1-16)	3	(0.4-8)	4.5	(0.4-16)
V. labrusca	31	(13)	11	(3-30)	4	(1.6-10)	10	(1.6-13)
V. Berlandieri	—		6.5	(1.5-12.5)	4	(1.5-6)	6	(1.5-12.5)
V. riparia	37.5	(25-50)	3	(1-25)	—		12	(1-50)

[1]Includes *V. Bourguiniana.*

The contribution of *V. vinifera* tends to rise from stage one to stage three. There are 7 of the 33 second stage hybrids reported to have less than 50% vinifera, including primitive types as Humbert 3 and S.V. 1-72 and some better known varieties such as Chancellor and DeChaunac.

INTERSPECIFIC HYBRIDS FROM AROUND THE WORLD

A small fraction of the hybrids of France has received our attention. So also will only a fraction of the interspecific hybrids produced elsewhere be mentioned. Selected are those which have already proven valuable additions to viticulture and some, with unusual attributes, which have real possibilities for the future.

Goals of interspecific hybridization are to incorporate into a new variety the genetic characteristics which are not available within *V. vinifera*. Disease and insect resistance are often primary goals, but so too may be winter hardiness, pigment production in hot climates, and, for table grapes, the flavor of labrusca.

According to the O.I.V. (International Office of the Vine) in 1980 there were some 86 governmental stations around the world with projects on grape breeding. There is no indication which are doing interspecific hybridization. Let us look at a few.

Canada

At the Vineland, Ontario, Experiment Station, Ollie Bradt and currently Helen Fisher, have had an extended breeding program for wine grapes. The French hybrids have been used for over 30 years and 4 of 5 winegrape introductions have included at least one French hybrid parent. The most recent release, Veeblanc, is an example of a second stage hybrid, S 13053 x S.V. 14-287.

In British Columbia, L.G. Denby at the Summerland Research Station, introduced a wine/table variety, Sovereign Rose, which is the cross, Bath x Perle of Csaba. The wine has a flowery muscat aroma and should be pressed before fermentation. A residual sugar level of 2-5% is recommended.

Germany

In spite of West German laws prohibiting the use of hybrids in commercial wines, several of the wine institutes have produced large numbers of hybrid seedlings. Siegfriedrebe, introduced over 20 years ago from Geilweilerhof, has been tried with some interest in the U.S. Other hybrids from this Institute have been received with less enthusiasm by the wine experts.

Helmut Becker, of Geisenheim, has also produced a number of hybrids. Two of the cross Chancellor (S 7053) x Reisling, Gm 32258 and Gm 32458, have received excellent wine reports. Both will soon be available for trial in the U.S. Dr. Becker has expressed an attitude toward such hybrids that warrants a quotation: "We are convinced that interspecific hybridization will be fundamental to vine improvement."

Hungary

It may come as a surprise to learn that about one-third of the vines in

Hungary are the North American variety Othello. Most of the fruit of this variety does not go into commercial wine, but is made and consumed locally. Hardiness, good color and disease resistance contribute to the continued use of this variety.

For winter hardiness, Hungarian breeders have used *V. amurensis*, a cold tolerant species from North China, crossed with vinifera. One third generation hybrid from repeated back crosses to viniferas retains remarkable tolerance to low winter temperatures and the wine can not be distinguished from those of the area. Some of these hybrids also carry a hypersensitivity to downy mildew.

A second breeding strategy to incorporate downy mildew resistance is through the use of French hybrids x vinifera. At least one wine selection shows promise, but laws prohibit its commercial planting. A table grape variety, Perle de Zala (S. V. 12-375 x Perle de Csaba) has been released for commercial use.

Russia

Hybrids in Russia date back to the Russian Concord of N.I. Vavilov who also attempted to incorporate hardiness from *V. amurensis*. Presently at Yalta there is under development the Magarath hybrids, Seibel and Seyve-Villard hybrids crossed with vinifera. In addition to disease, insect resistance and high sugars, the wine quality of several is reported better than standard vinifera. Golvdriga states that "one can no longer be unaware that these new hybrids are not inferior in quality to the European varieties" and suggests the term "complex hybrids" to indicate their superiority relative to the older hybrid direct producers.

U.S.A.

With the exception of much of the grape breeding in California, almost all of the varieties originated in the U.S. have been interspecific hybrids. I shall restrict this discussion to grapes which were originated primarily for wine use or have proven adapted to wine use in spite of the breeder's goal to develop a table grape.

The grape breeders of the U.S. have available both the gene pool of native species and the best of earlier hybrids produced by pioneer breeders such as T.V. Munson of Texas, and Herman Jaeger of Missouri.

California. The high temperatures of the interior valleys of California depress the pigment levels of red viniferas. Salvador, apparently one of the Seibel hybrids, has been grown there, but its pigments have a violet cast.

H.P Olmo crossed Alicante Ganzin [(Aramon x *V. rupestris*) x Alicante)] with Trousseau and with Mourisco preto. From the first cross he originated Royalty; from the second, Rubired. Thus both are interspecific hybrids and carry $^1/_8$ *V. rupestris* ancestry. There are now over 10,000 acres of Rubired in California.

At present there is a research project which may lead to protoplast fusion in *Vitis*. This could allow genes for resistance to disease or insects to be inserted into a variety without the generations of crossing and selection involved with conventional breeding of grapes.

Florida. The limiting factor of *Euvitis* in Florida is Pierce's Disease, a bacterial wilt. *Euvitis* species native to Florida, about which there is considerable disagreement on names, are tolerant to Pierce's Disease and have been crossed both with American varieties and French hybrids at the Leesburg Station by Loren Stover and John Mortensen. A half-dozen introductions provide the area with grapes that survive and can be vinified for lack of all else except muscadines.

Mississippi. There has been a revival of interest in wine grapes supported by an enology program at the State University. From a USDA grape breeding program at Meridian which was terminated in 1965, several breeding lines selected for survival in the presence of Pierce's Disease have been maintained at the State University. Recently, two of these which survived the disease pressures and were reasonably productive were named for release and trial in the area. Skillful vinification will be required to produce a quality wine.

Missouri. Under the direction of the late Paul Shepard, several fruit breeding programs were carried on at the Mountain Grove experiment station. A baker's dozen of table grapes were introduced in 1947, several of which were Concord type which, it was hoped, would substitute for Concord which does not ripen evenly there.

One of these was named for a small town in southern Missouri, Blue Eye. The flavor is Concord-like and it has found some favor in Ohio for a varietal wine. While the wine is foxy, the pigments are of the vinifera type and its hybrid origin can not be demonstrated by chromatography.

Another of Shepard's introductions is St. Francis, a cross of Munson's Muench (Neosho x Herbemont) x Danugue (a giant clustered vinifera table grape). The St. Francis is thus free of any labrusca inheritance and has made some pleasant wine in the central Atlantic states.

New York. A breeding program for table grapes has been operating for almost a century and many of the successful table grapes of the east originated from the Geneva station. Interest in wine grapes has been supported by the wineries of the state for the last 25 years and a wine project has enabled the breeders to select seedlings suitable for wine.

The first wine grape introduction, Cayuga White (Seyval x Schuyler) was named in 1972. Several selections, available for testing through the New York State Fruit Testing Cooperative at Geneva, are modern hybrid type crosses. GW-8 is Pinot blanc x Auroré. GW-9 and GW-10 are Seyval x Chardonnay. Several more recent selections, both red and white, are under investigation and may be made available for trial.

Cooperation between the breeder and plant pathologist to identify powdery mildew resistance may lead to selections with sufficient resistance to this disease to reduce need for special sprays.

North Carolina. Grape breeding, primarily muscadines, has been under way for almost three-quarters of a century at North Carolina State University. For the past fifteen years there has been a promising evolution in the program. Bunch grape breeding, fertile hybrids between bunch grapes and muscadines, under Bill Nesbitt, plus a winemaking program under Dan Carroll, should make possible the development of varieties specifically for wine-use adapted to this climate.

Other States. Other programs still active or recently terminated at experiment stations in Arkansas, Georgia, Maryland, South Carolina, South Dakota and Virginia plus an extensive and enthusiastic coterie of amateur breeders give further promise of useful interspecific hybrids.

SUMMARY

The desire to grow grapes is not limited to these favored geographical areas well suited to the culture of *Vitis vinifera*. Where the vinifera varieties fail or economic risk becomes intolerable, interspecific hybrids of many sorts become acceptable. Over the two and one-half centuries that interspecific hybrids have been grown, the rate of improvement in quality has been astounding.

We have seen a winnowing out of some species, as the discrimination against *V. labrusca* and *V. riparia*, in the evolution of the French hybrids. More recently there has been a selection for individual attributes available only from wild species, such as downy mildew resistance or winter hardiness, by repeated backcrosses to vinifera. This refects the attitude that the wine quality of the hybrids must approach the quality of pure vinifera varieties while giving the grower the advantage of lower risks.

Conventional breeding will continue to give new hybrids of better wine quality or tougher hybrids to further extend the area where grapes can be grown. The techniques of tissue culture and genetic engineering may someday make possible undreamed of combinations.

CHAPTER SEVEN

SEX AND THE SINGLE VINE

By John R. McGrew, PhD.

T HE INCEPTION of this chapter was the visualization in the American Wine Society Journal of a larger-than-life, explicit, full-color centerfold of a grape flower cluster in full bloom. (Editor's Note: The author finally settled for non-folding, black and white photos.)

There are other reasons (other than prurience) for the grape grower and wine drinker to be aware of the sex life of a grapevine. This sex life is complicated in some respects, but generally successful enough that there is wine for the table without any attention from us. In the beginning, however, this was not so.

We will never know where or when man first planted a vineyard. Indeed, we can never be sure why it was planted, whether in anticipation of fruit for eating fresh or raisins or wine.

We can assume that in the beginning, wine was not the major reason for growing grapes. The end product of natural fermentation is not wine but vinegar. Those who tended the fermentation would need fine judgement for the fleeting moments when the alcoholic content was optimum. The brew would have to have been consumed promptly and there was no reason to make large quantities.

Eventually through improved skills of the potter and exclusion of air by means of a fitted cap or layer of olive oil, wine would be held for longer periods. It became practical to make more wine than could be consumed in a brief bacchanal.

Some fruit could be collected from wild vines that grew in most areas where man first settled down from a stone-age hunter-gatherer life. In order to improve the source of supply the primitive farmer applied the same logic to the vine that had succeeded in the domestication of grain and pulse crops.

The grower who planted seeds or who took cuttings at random from wild vines succeeded reasonably well. The careful husbandman who marked the choicest vines at harvest and used cuttings or layers only from these to set his vineyard failed. Here sex rears its head.

The wild vines of *Vitis* have either male or female flowers. The grower who used seedlings or unselected cuttings planted both sexes in the vineyard. The careful grower might find a berry or two where pollen had blown in from distant male vines, but the vine did not respond to cultivation as had other, more docile crops. The inclusion of non-productive male-flowered vines in the ancient vineyards was as necessary as pollinator trees among date palms.

At some time during the first few thousand years of interest in and attempts to plant vineyards, a spontaneous mutation of flower type occurred that allowed the vine to be domesticated. This was the appearance of vines with self-fertile flowers. The vineyards where these vines grew were free of the need for stud vines. This characteristic is transmitted genetically, so some of the daughter vines are also self-fruitful. Thus, the new flower type could be incorporated into other and better varieties suited to solid-set vineyards long before the reason for success was understood.

Figure 1a
The sex of a vine can be recognized by looking at the flower during the first day or so after the cap has fallen off. The male (staminate) flower has five upright, straight stamens carrying five anthers (pollen sacs). There is, at most, a rudimentary pistil.

Figure 1b
In the female (pistilate) flower, the stamens are relaxed, curved backwards and down. There are anthers with some pollen, but the pollen is not fertile. This pistil is functional with a rounded ovule. The stile extends upward surmounted by the pollen-receptive stigma.

Figure 1c
The self-fertile (perfect) flower combines the upright stamens of the male and the developed pistil of the female flowers.

There are other (secondary) differences between the growth and flowering patterns of wild vines. Male-flowered vines that need produce only pollen have much larger clusters with many times more flowers. There are more clusters per flowering shoot. The appearance of a male vine in full flower is one of exuberant procreativity, the flowers almost hiding the foliage (Figure 2). There is also a tendency for the male vines to flower throughout the growing season. This loading of the aircurrents with massive quantities of pollen improves the chances of successful pollination of female vines.

The flower clusters of female vines (Figure 3) are smaller, fewer in number and vines generally have only a single blossoming each year.

There are three genes involved in the control of sexual expression in the vine flowers. Staminate is genetically dominate over the self-fertile mutation which in turn is dominate over pistilate. The permutations of the 36 possible genetic combinations and the segregation of sexes in progeny populations are understood, but are of concern primarily to the grape breeder.

Besides the vineyard success of solid planted self-fertile vines, there was another result from the appearance of this mutation. One could remove the non-productive male vines without loss of crop on the fruitful vines. The suppression of male vines actually eliminated the gene for male flowers from the cultivated vine at some time before the oldest recorded instructions on vine culture. The male vinifera exists today only as wild vines in its area of origination of Asia Minor and a few glacial-refuge areas of Europe.

Because the gene for female flowers is recessive, it exists covertly within the population. Female-flowered vines do appear regularly as chance seedlings and in the progenies of experimental crosses. There are a few minor commercial varieties with pistilate flowers, but, as did the ancient wild female-flowered vines, they require pollen from another variety and are subject to irregular crops. Except for many rootstock varieties, all of the popular cultivated varieties of grapes, whether pure vinifera, hybrids or American types, are self-fertile. Only a few of the older muscadines, as "Scuppernong", and an occasional special purpose grape, as the very early vinifera table grape "Madelaine Angevine" or the Pierces Disease tolerant "Norris" require pollinators.

The original mutation for perfect flowers is thought to have occurred in a male-flowered vine. Occasionally a wild male vine will set a berry or two with fertile seeds. The genetic information for production of both sexes is carried by, although generally suppressed in, the male vine. The mutation released the development of functional pistils along with the normal stamens in a single vine.

This hypothetical origin is strengthened by the larger and more numerous clusters often found on perfect-flowered vines (Figure 4). These male attributes were carried along with the new flower type. It also explains why vines must be pruned to control crop size. The wild female vines evolved for both perpetuation of the species and survival of the individual without the interference of man. The new perfect-flowered vines were potentially self-destructive through uncontrolled overproduction of fruit, and therefore required the skilled hand of the vigneron to assure their survival.

Another advantage in the new vines was the carrying along of the reblooming character of wild male vines. This provides insurance against complete loss of the annual crop from late spring frosts and is found in many, though not all, perfect-flowered varieties.

Among the older varieties of *V. vinifera*, some balance between fruitfulness and overfruitfulness has been established through centuries of selection. In the hybrid direct producers (French hybrids), because of their recent return to characteristics of maleness from the influx of genes from the North American species, we see the potential for excessive production and rebloom.

Had not the vine itself achieved a spontaneous and major adaptation in its sex life and the origination of self-fertile flowers, cultivation of the grape as it has existed for several thousand years might have failed. Wine would not have become an attribute and enjoyment of civilization, but would have been found among more primitive peoples who could collect the fruit of wild vines and brew a substitute beverage for the Beers of Bacchus.

Chapter Eight

BLACK ROT

By John R. McGrew, PhD.

Bᴌᴀᴄᴋ ʀᴏᴛ can be controlled sufficiently well that it is seldom a major problem, but most growers see some every year and occasionally far more than that. A grower will be able to control black rot more effectively when the interrelationships among the various players in this game are understood. There are a few basic rules which will be listed first.

1. The host:

All cultivated varieties are susceptible to infection by the black rot fungus. However, one of the keys to control of this disease is that only the immature portions of a grapevine are susceptible. Once the tissues reach full size, they become immune from infection by this fungus. If a leaf escapes infection for the 5 to 10 days it needs to reach full size, it will then be safe.

The economic damage from black rot is the loss of fruit. The above rule holds for fruit, but berries require several weeks, not days, to reach full size. Thus, the developing berries are at risk for a longer period than the leaves. It is of no concern to the fungus whether it attacks leaves or fruit; it just seems to prefer the fruit.

2. The causal organism:

Guignardia bidwellii is the fungus that causes black rot. It is endemic on wild vines throughout the eastern U.S. There are two kinds of spores produced. One kind can travel a considerable distance; the more common summer spores (conidia) are moved only by the slashing of rain. Neither spore has any power of motility and are at the mercy of the elements.

3. Conditions for spore germination:

Free water on the surface of the vine is necessary for germination of the spores. At 80°F, spores will germinate in as little as 6 hours. At higher and lower temperatures germination may take up to 24 hours.

4. Infection:

When a spore germinates on susceptible vine tissue, infection is rapid. The mycelium of the germinating spore penetrates a vine cell and begins feeding on that and adjacent vine cells. For 5 days or more the fungus can continue to spread inside the vine cells without causing any visible symptoms.

Figure 1   *Figure 2*

5. Symptoms:

After a period of 1 to 3 weeks, depending on temperature and variety, a tan necrotic lesion with a dark margin (Figure 1) develops where the infection was established. In another 3 to 5 days the typical tiny, black fruiting structures (pycnidia) of the fungus appear and mature in the central area. The numbers range from as few as a half-dozen in a small leaf lesion to several hundred on an infected berry (Figure 2). If a leaf is one day short of fully expanded when infected, the fungus has only one day to spread and the lesion is small. If the leaf is 10 days short of fully expanded, the fungus continues to grow and produces a relatively large lesion.

6. Release of summer spores:

When a mature pycnidium becomes wet, the contents swell and conidia are released. Rain can splash them onto susceptible tissues and new infections occur.

7. Infection cycle:

The sequence of the release of conidia, dispersal, germination, infection, to the development of a new lesion with mature pycnidia is an *infection cycle* and it takes from 10 to 20 days. Each growing season is long enough to allow the stringing together of several infection cycles that permits black rot to build up to disastrous levels. But even without fungicides, most infection cycles will not approach their full potential for increase. The home-owner with a single unsprayed vine of Concord will some years harvest a full crop. Similarly, a skilled grower who sprays regularly will some years see a trace of black rot explode in a single infection cycle to a significant loss of fruit.

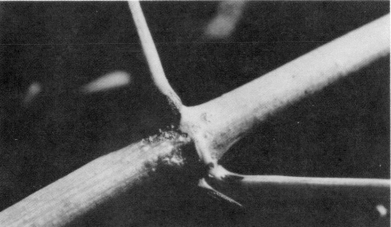

Figure 3

Figure 4

THE ANNUAL CYCLE

At this point we turn to an outline of black rot development throughout the growing season.

There are two possible sources of the first lesion in a vineyard. The usual is from a lesion formed the previous growing season. The fungus can overwinter in lesions on fruiting canes (Figure 3), tendrils (Figure 4) or cluster parts left on the vine. The more black rot last year, the greater the chance that lesions will be present in suitable locations to restart the disease early in the growing season.

The other source of first lesions is the sexual stage of the fungus. A black rot infected cluster that is dropped on the ground at harvest time can produce sexual spores (ascospores). These develop in the same fruiting structures (now called perithecia) and are sets of 8 ascospores formed inside a tube-like structure (ascus). When a mature ascus becomes wet, the contents swell and the individual spores are forcibly discharged. Once airborne they can travel for a considerable distance.

Ascospores from wild vines in the tops of trees anywhere upwind are the usual source of black rot in a young vineyard or one previously free of black rot. In cooler areas the timing of ascospore discharge is often well coordinated with young, susceptible foliage in the vineyard. Further south, discharge may occur during warm periods before growth begins in the vineyard. However, eventually the weather will allow ascospores to drift in at the appropriate stage of shoot growth to start an infection.

Whatever the source, we now have a typical leaf lesion in the vineyard. Scattered through the central area of the lesion are the pycnidia which are flask-like and have a small opening at the surface of the leaf. Each contains thousands of summer spores (conidia). Within 15 seconds of becoming wet, the absorbed moisture causes the contents to swell and the spores are squeezed out like toothpaste. Spores may continue to be released for 3 to 5 minutes. There is the potential for an astronomical increase in the amount of vineyard infection.

The particular weather conditions that initiate an infection cycle play a major role in determining the effectiveness of that cycle. Rain will splash these conidia about in a random manner. In the following scenarios we will say that there is a new crop of mature pycnidia and no fungicide on the vines to inhibit spore germination and thus prevent infection.

Consider that instead of a rain shower, there is a heavy dew. The moisture will release the conidia which will not splash anywhere and can not themselves move to susceptible tissue. They stay right there and germinate. The surrounding tissue is mature and there is no infection. The first crop of conidia from a pycnidia is the big one. A few days later a smaller second crop may be available.

Given a gentle rain shower: The conidia are released, washed to tissues below the original lesion. Some will land on susceptible tissues and there will be a few new lesions. But consider that only perhaps 5% of the vine surface is susceptible, 95% of the conidia which do land on the vine are going to fail to establish a new infection. Also, most of the rain, and the conidia contained in it, will land on the vineyard floor.

Given a brief, harder rain, without wind, followed by high humidity for 24 hours: Some conidia may be splashed out or even upwards, as well as down. These conditions favor the fungus. Add a strong wind and some conidia may be moved to adjacent vines. This approaches the worst scenario.

Given the same brief, hard rain, but followed by a drying wind: Through luck or selection of a good, windy vineyard site, if the film of water drys within 6 hours, there may be little or no infection. But if the conidia are rewetted within 3 days, they can still cause an infection. Also, in spite of the wind, it is possible for free water to remain trapped among berries in the cluster long enough for infection.

Given an extended downpour, with wind, the conidia are given as wide a distribution as is possible, but the continued rain can wash most of them off the vines before they can germinate.

In all these examples, the percentage of conidia that produce new lesions is miniscule. For the fungus, success is production of two new lesions from an original single lesion.

The role of the vineyardist is to reduce the potential of each infection cycle. A fungicide applied just before a rain will be effective provided it has time to dry and stick. It will protect all the susceptible tissues it covers. With increasing time between spray application and an infection cycle, more new susceptible tissues will develop beyond the area protected. A week to 10 days after a spray, all the sprayed foliage will have become naturally immune and all the new susceptible leaves will be unprotected.

With the advent of triadimefon (Bayleton) and more recent related systemic fungicides, a new and powerful control technique has become available to the grape grower. (Benlate, even though a systemic, is not included among these as it is not effective against black rot.) Ferbam, maneb, captan and the other standard non-systemic fungicides can not follow the fungus into the vine cells after infection. The systemics can, and if applied before the fungus has had time to kill many of the vine cells, within 72 hours, can eradicate potential infections.

BERRY INFECTIONS

Once the berries begin to form, the greater the number of lesions present at the moment rain starts, the greater the chance that random slashing will carry infection to a cluster of fruit. If a berry is infected early in the season, two or more successive infection cycles can occur within a single cluster. Conidia produced on an infected berry are in an ideal location to infect other berries in the same cluster.

Figure 5

The first symptom on a berry is a soft, circular brown area which enlarges in one or two days to involve the entire berry. This happens because young berries are several weeks from maturity. A single point of infection can continue to grow and destroy the entire berry. As the berry begins to shrivel, pycnidia develop over the entire berry surface. After 2 or 3 more days the berry will blacken and dry. It usually remains firmly attached to the cluster. (Figure 5)

Berries are more difficult to protect with fungicides than foliage, beyond the fact that they remain susceptible for a much longer period. As they expand, any fungicide that has stuck to them is diluted over the greater surface area. It is just as difficult for rain water trapped among berries to evaporate as it is to get fungicides into the cluster. Again, the systemic fungicides can eradicate berry infections if applied within 72 hours of the start of an infection cycle.

The berries remain susceptible to black rot only until they reach full size. This means that Concord will become immune in about 5 weeks. Given the 2 weeks between infection and symptoms, any berry free of black rot at 7 weeks is home free, so far as black rot is concerned. Late season varieties, especially viniferas, may remain susceptible up to 4 weeks longer and require extended protection.

CONTROL

With the timely use of systemic fungicides to correct for lapses in protection from standard fungicides, it may now be possible to achieve perfect control of black rot. It is debatable whether this intensive spraying is practical, cost effective, or even necessary. Even with complete suppression of black rot this year, one must spray next year to protect against the possibility of ascospores drifting in.

There are differences in susceptibility to black rot among varieties, but none combine sufficient resistance to eliminate the need for spraying with a quality of fruit suitable for wine. The anecdotal reports of a variety which is "especially" susceptible are often based on an area of a vineyard in which black rot has built up to such a level that it is difficult to control. In one vineyard variety A is "susceptible" and variety B is "resistant", while in another vineyard the two may be reversed.

Knowledge of how this disease works suggests several general recommendations for control.

1. Minimize the effectiveness of the first infection cycle by reducing overwintering inoculum. The best way to do this is by good control of black rot the previous year. When the vineyard is pruned, do not leave black-rotted clusters hanging on the vine or lying in the vineyard. The avid hobbyist with a few vines should remove tendrils from the wires or push them to the posts away from the area of new growth. If black rot was severe the previous year, care should be taken to select fruiting wood without stem lesions.

2. The early sprays are the most important. As midseason approaches, less time is left for successive infection cycles to build up to damaging levels. Whether or not you see black rot lesions in the early spring, do not put off spraying. The spray schedules are designed to control other fungus diseases and omission of "black rot" sprays may allow other problems to develop.

3. The basic fungicide in the spray program should be one of the standard, non-systemic ones. The systemic fungicides should be reserved for the situations when a spray was missed or for unusual conditions where eradication is required.

4. Given any options, spray with a standard fungicide before a rain. If it rains 3 to 7 days after such a spray, based on the amount of black rot in the vineyard, consider an extra eradicant spray with a systemic fungicide.

CHAPTER NINE

CROWN GALLS AND WINTER INJURY

By Herman O. Amberg

IN HIS ARTICLE "A Visit To Some East Coast Vineyards" (American Wine Society Journal, Fall 1991), Professor R. Bernard of France mentions "the essential problem, of annual winter damage to the favored varieties . . ."

He associates this with sites which are scarcely suitable for grape growing, and also with "the frequent presence in large quantity of *broussins* (Crown gall tumors)," which occur here after temperatures have fallen to $-20°$ to $-25°$ C ($-5°$ to $-12°$ F), and which are rare in France.

The same approximate point of vulnerability prevails in German vineyards. Professor W. Hillebrand of Bad Kreuznach in varietal descriptions has written: "frequent minimum temperatures below $-5°$ F make winter cold injury unavoidable."

Let us compare the average minimum temperatures of Germany with those of the northeastern United States:

At Geisenheim (Rhine) and Bernkastel (Mosel)	$+9°$ F
At Geneva, New York	$-7°$ F
The difference is	$-16°$ F

What this difference says is that with fair success we are growing *vinifera* varieties at or below the low margin of the German temperature range. How do we do this?

As Professor Bernard points out, good site selection and sound vineyard management are the keys to success in Germany. The same is true in the northeastern U.S.

In New York State a good vinifera site is located below 800′ elevation, with a slope toward east, south or west of 5% or more and a drainage area for cold air below. A large body of open water to the west is advantageous. So much for site selection.

As for sound vineyard management, that is achieved when the leaf area is well exposed, at a density expressed by a pruning weight of .3 to .4 pounds of prunings per running foot of row, with shoot growth ceasing in mid-August and maturing a crop of 3-4 tons per acre.

To achieve this goal, rootstock vigor has to be matched with soil fertility, vine spacing, appropriate fertilization, good soil management and, in some circumstances, summer pruning. During the winter months a portion of the trunk above the graft union requires protection; and it is now generally accepted that multiple trunks are a desirable form of insurance, since in case of severe trunk damage they provide a source of trunk renewal.

It is also taken for granted that in winters when temperatures fall below −10° F even the hardiest *vinifera* varieties, such as Chardonnay and Riesling, will suffer winter cold injury.

As for winter cold injury, a distinction must be made between two kinds. There is bud injury, which is usually compensated for by retaining a surplus of buds and adjusting when the amount of injury has been determined. And then there is trunk injury, which varies greatly and can be critical for the survival of the trunk and indeed of the vine.

Having closely observed *vinifera* varieties over the past 34 years, I now define three different levels of winter trunk injury — all of them related to the severity of injury to the cambium layer. The cambium tissue is the only growing tissue in a trunk. It is located between the bark (phloem) and the wood (xylem). It produces new bark and new wood every season, the latter being evident in the well-known yearly rings.

Injury Level #1.   This shows as a browning of part or most of the phloem layer in early spring. It is usually not recognized, because it rarely becomes visible on the outside of the trunks. But occasionally when there has been a limited degree of cambium injury, the healing process of bridging the dead tissue with new callus may show up as moderate tumor tissue outside the bark. After a season or two this wound tissue will be shed with the bark and the trunk is intact again.

Injury Level #2 is the familiar and dreaded degree of injury. After considerable browning, which is to say killing, of phloem tissue, vine growth in the spring appears to be normal. But later in the season narrow sectors or whole plates of the bark dry up and crown gall tumors may appear. What has happened is that surviving cambium sectors have been unable to bridge the gap over damaged sectors and reach the nearest neighboring callus growth. As a result the affected trunk areas either dry up or develop galls which will die in time too. The injury to the trunk is permanent.

Trunks with **Level #2** injury may survive several seasons with declining crop production. But if trunk renewal from below the affected area is not , or can not, be carried out, the vine is doomed.

Injury Level #3. This is the most severe degree of injury. More extensive brown phloem tissue can be observed. Coming out of dormancy there may be be some bleeding and a beginning of shoot growth. But during the summer months shoots from above the area of injury become stunted and finally collapse. The assumption is that with this degree of injury the cambium layer was killed and therefore the healing process could not start. The trunks are quite free of tumors and are dead.

At injury **Level #3** a vine can not survive unless another of its multiple trunks has received less injury, or else new shoots can be brought up from below the damaged area and be used for trunk renewal. Occasionally, such shoots emerge from the rootstock, below the graft union, and hence are worthless. The reason for the numerous successful *vinifera* operations can be found in the adherence to the described practices.

The prevailing assumption has been that if crown gall could be eliminated the winter hardiness of grapevines, and their ability to recover from winter injury, would be improved. Working on that assumption recent researchers have succeeded in shedding more light on the crown gall problem and the bacterium *(Agrobacterium tumefaciens)* that is the cause. They assert that only one of the many strains of this bacterium, known as Biovar 3, is responsible for the tumor development.

This bacterium can be isolated from the bleeding sap and tissue of *all commercial sources of grape material*. It is inactive in healthy tissue, but begins its cancerous activity at some points in the healing process of vines with severe cambium injury as described in **Injury Level #2.** Such damage is caused most frequently by low winter temperatures, but can also be of mechanical origin. The cancerous character of the tumor tissue has been demonstrated, but this does not necessarily interfere with the healing process at the wound.

I conclude that the frequent development of crown galls on grapes *is the result of severe trunk injury,* not the cause of it. The galls are so abundant on *vinifera* simply because our pattern of winter temperatures so frequently falls below their tolerance level.

In any case, the effort to develop "clean" propagating material continues, meaning vines free of the villanous Biovar 3. And looking beyond such a successful accomplishment they discuss regulatory control of propagating material and plant sites together with the usual bureaucratic apparatus. Presently, I know of no solid evidence that any planting of supposedly "clean" vines has shown itself more tolerant of winter cold injury, or shown greater ability to heal severe injury, than current commercial material.

CHAPTER TEN

FIELD GRAFTING IN COLD CLIMATE VINEYARDS

By Arthur C. Hunt

**A Method For Rapidly And Economically Converting
From One Variety To Another In A Mature Vineyard.**

BECAUSE OF constantly changing market environment, certain wines and consequently, certain grape varieties, come into and out of favor. Field grafting is a method of changing varieties in a mature vineyard by cutting off an old vine and grafting scions (cuttings) of a new variety onto the old trunk.

In California, field grafting has been successfully performed on a commercial basis for many years. However, because of the severe winter temperatures in the Finger Lakes, previous field grafting attempts have been either unsuccessful or not commercially practical.

In 1979 and 1980, Dr. Thomas Zabadal, Co-operative Extension Regional Grape Specialist in the Finger Lakes, began investigating the possibility of adapting California techniques to the cold climate grapes. He worked with a California group one spring and studied their methods. Dr. Zabadal developed techniques to slow the growth rates of the new scion shoots. This, in turn, enabled the new shoots to grow in a balanced fashion and to properly mature in the fall to withstand the severe winters.

Those techniques included various vine configurations such as leaving renewals, or decapitating one side of a two-trunk vine. Another technique was to slash the trunk below the graft to prevent flooding of the scion by sap flow. The goal is to change from one variety to another rapidly, consistently and economically.

In 1981 and 1982, Dr. Zabadal grafted several dozen vines successfully, which encouraged him to experiment on a larger basis.

Because my name was on several legislative mailing lists, I heard about a USDA program for small business innovative research grants to small, "for-profit" businesses. Dr. Zabadal and I together successfully applied for a grant, with Hunt Farms as the small business and Dr. Zabadal as the consultant.

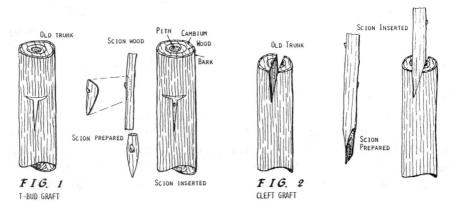

Figure 1

Figure 2

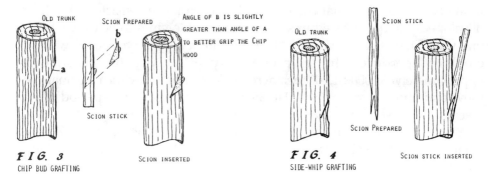

Figure 3

Figure 4

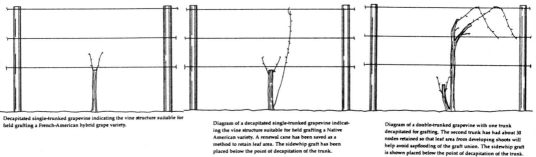

Decapitated single-trunked grapevine indicating the vine structure suitable for field grafting a French-American hybrid grape variety.

Diagram of a decapitated single-trunked grapevine indicating the vine structure suitable for field grafting a Native American variety. A renewal cane has been saved as a method to retain leaf area. The sidewhip graft has been placed below the point of decapitation of the trunk.

Diagram of a double-trunked grapevine with one trunk decapitated for grafting. The second trunk has had about 30 nodes retained so that leaf area from developing shoots will help avoid sapflooding of the graft union. The sidewhip graft is shown placed below the point of decapitation of the trunk.

Figure 5

Figure 6

Figure 7

In 1984, the first year of the program, we investigated about 40 different combinations of grafting techniques, varietal combinations and vine configurations. We tried six different grafting techniques, including sidewhip (Figure 4), wedge, t-bud (Figure 1), chip (Figure 3), bark and greenshoot grafts. We also repeated the trials at four different times in the spring. Several thousand vines were involved.

The following year, with a matching grant from the New York State Science and Technology Foundation, we narrowed the field to the 10 most promising combinations and added cleft grafting (Figure 4). We included more varietal combinations, and the results were rather encouraging. Some of our more successful trials were 96 to 99% successful. We also began to learn how to tailor the most appropriate technique to any given vine scenario.

With additional funding from USDA, we are working with seedless table grapes as well as wine varieties, and now are trying to optimize the regrowth of the post-grafted vines.

1987 is the fourth and last year of this project, and we hope to further refine the process, so that the regrowth is even more consistent. We have developed practical procedures which will enable vines to be converted in one year. That is, graft Variety "B" onto Variety "A" in year one (with no crop), and produce a full crop of Variety "B" in year two. The cost is approximately $1,000-$1,200 per acre. This compares with a normal (remove and replant) cost of $4,000 to $5,000 per acre and a time period of 5 to 7 years.

Who would be willing to guess what variety will be in vogue 7 years from now? But, we might be able to look 2 or 3 years ahead a bit more confidently.

For many vineyards, field grafting may become the most practical and economical method for changing varieties. Our aim is to make this information available to all who may wish to use the technology. Accordingly, Dr. Zabadal has written an in-depth, two-part article with many full color photographs, originally published in the August-September and October-November 1985 issues of *Eastern Grape Grower* magazine (now *Vineyard & Winery Management* magazine). Reprint copies are available at a cost of $4.00 by writing to: Dr. Thomas Zabadal, Yates County Cooperative Extension Service, 110 Court Street, Penn Yan, New York 14418.

BOOKS WITH INFORMATION ON VINICULTURE

Galet, Pierre. *A PRACTICAL AMPELOGRAPHY.* Translated and adapted by Lucie T. Morton. Cornell University Press. Ithaca 1979.

Morton, Lucie T. *WINEGROWING IN EASTERN AMERICA.* Cornell University Press. Ithaca. 1985

Pearson, Roger C. and Goheen, Austin C. *COMPENDIUM OF GRAPE DISEASES.* APS Press. St. Paul. 1988. ˉ

Robinson, Jancis. *VINES, GRAPES AND WINES.* Alfred A. Knopf. New York. 1986.

Wagner, Philip M. *A WINE-GROWER'S GUIDE.* Third Edition. Revised; Alfred A. Knopf. 1984.

Weaver, Robert J. *GRAPE GROWING.* John Wiley & Sons. New York. 1976.

Winkler, A.J. *GENERAL VITICULTURE.* University of California Press. Berkeley. 1975.

Pamphlets

Cattell, H. and Stauffer, H.L. *THE WINES OF THE EAST: THE HYBRIDS.* L & H Photojournalism. Lancaster, PA 1978.

THE WINES OF THE EAST: NATIVE AMERICAN GRAPES. L & H Photojournalism. Lancaster, PA. 1980.

THE WINES OF THE EAST: THE VINIFERA. L & H Photojournalism. Lancaster, PA. 1979.

Jordan, T.D. , Pool, R.M., Tomkins, J.P., and Zabadal, T.J. *CULTURAL PRACTICES FOR COMMERCIAL VINEYARDS.* Miscellaneous Bulletin 111. New York State College of Agriculture and Life Sciences, Cornell University. Ithaca. 1981.

A GUIDE TO AMERICAN AND FRENCH HYBRID GRAPE VARIETIES. Foster Nursery Co. Inc. P.O. Box 150, Fredonia, NY 14063.

Periodicals

AMERICAN FRUIT GROWER. Willoughby, OH 44094

AMERICAN JOURNAL OF ENOLOGY AND VITICULTURE. American Society of Enology and Viticulture, P.O. Box 411, Davis, CA 95616.

AMERICAN WINE SOCIETY JOURNAL. 3006 Latta Rd., Rochester, NY 14612

CALIFORNIA AND WESTERN STATES GRAPE GROWER. 4974 E. Clinton Way, Suite 123, Fresno, CA 93727

GREAT LAKES FRUIT GROWERS NEWS. 343 South Union Street, P.O. Box 128, Sparta, MI 49345

PRACTICAL WINERY & VINEYARD. 15 Grand Paseo, San Rafael, CA 94903

VINIFERA WINE GROWERS JOURNAL. 1947 Hillside Drive, Stroudsburg, PA 18360

VINEYARD & WINERY MANAGEMENT. Box 231, Watkins Glen, NY Publishes annual supplier's guide.

WINE EAST. 620 North Pine Street, Lancaster, PA 17603. Publishes annual supplier's guide.

WINES AND VINES. 1800 Lincoln Avenue, San Rafael, CA 94901-1298. Publishes annual supplier's guide.

SUPPLIES

Pesticides

A pesticide applicators permit, issued by each state through the County Agent, may be required to purchase some of the materials that make the grape grower's life easier and more productive. Less toxic insecticides and fungicides sufficient to control most pests will usually be available without a permit.

Spray Equipment

A quart per vine is the estimate for good spray coverage on a small planting, 12 vines per 3 gallon sprayerful. Somewhere around 50 vines you will wish for a small power sprayer. An acre requires 150-250 gallons and you are into the $500 plus class of spray rigs.

Spraying and Spray Materials

Today's grape grower has an advantage over those thirsty souls whose grapes have been withering on the vines since the early Colonial days. We now know what causes the troubles and we have an arsenal of effective spray materials.

For less than 10 vines, it is probably more economical to use one of the proprietary fruit spray mixtures. Be sure grapes are listed on the labels.

For more vines, bags or bottles of individual spray materials will be less expensive per unit weight and you can apply only those materials needed in each spray. Many states publish an annual spray calendar for home fruit gardens and/or commercial grape growers. These will recommend specific fungicides and insecticides and will give optimum dates of application. Unfortunately, many are geared to the natural resistance of Concord rather than hybrids or viniferas.

Bird Control

Netting 12' to 18' wide draped over a trellis gives good protection against birds. It is easy to put on and difficult to remove as the vine shoots and tendrils tangle in it. If the trellis posts are extended about 2' with 2 X 2's and the tops of these interconnected with heavy twine or light wire, a 50 foot wide net can cover 4 or 5 rows and can give excellent protection if the edges are pegged down. Initial investment is high, but the netting should last 5 to 10 years.

Cheesecloth or used tobacco shade cloth casts considerable shade (lower sugar), retains humidity (ripe rots), and must be amortized in one season. Scare devices have limited effectiveness or high local nuisance levels. Nearby neighbors do not take kindly to cannon fire or screaming banshees at 5:00 a.m. on a Sunday morning.

Miscellaneous Supplies

Local hardware stores, large mail-order houses and such may be able to supply pruning shears, string, wire, wire tighteners, sprayers, etc. One source for a wide range of pruners, plastic ties, tying machines, etc. is A.M. Leonard, Inc., P.O. Box 816, Piqua, OH 45356. Others are: Growers Supply Center, 2415 Harford Road, Fallston, MD 21047, (301) 529-7161; Orchard Valley Supply, RD #1, Box 41-B, Fawn Grove, PA 17321, (717) 382-4612.

JOIN THE AMERICAN WINE SOCIETY

The American Wine Society is a national non-profit consumer organization devoted to educating its members and the general public about all aspects of wine-production, use and appreciation. The society is independent and has no commercial affiliation.

The Society publishes a quarterly Journal containing articles on all aspects of wine appreciation, grape growing, and winemaking, Society news, local Chapter news, book reviews and recipes.

Local American Wine Society Chapters have activities such as wine tastings, luncheons, dinners, picnics, lectures, amateur winemaking contests, tours, etc. Each year in November a $2^1/2$ day national wine conference offers an opportunity for members to come together and learn more about wine.

Membership is open to any interested person; wine enthusiast, professional in the wine business, amateur winemaker — anyone who wants to learn more about wine. All members receive the quarterly American Wine Society Journal, invitations to attend local, regional and national events, and new technical manuals when they are published. Annual dues are $32.00 per individual or couple. For those who join after July 1, and do not wish to receive the full year's publications, dues are $18.00.

Application for membership in The American Wine Society

Complete and mail with your check to:

AMERICAN WINE SOCIETY
3006 LATTA ROAD
ROCHESTER, NY 14612
(716) 225-7613

Last Name   First Name   Initial

Name of spouse (if applicable)

Street or Route number

City   State   Zip Code

Area Code / Phone   Member's Signature

Check type membership which applies to you:

☐ Regular membership (calendar year) (per couple or individual) (US$) $32.00

☐ After July 1 ($^1/_2$ year) $18.00

☐ Professional membership (includes wall plaque and special listings) $52.00

☐ Spousal voting privileges $ 2.00

☐ Canada and Mexico add $ 6.00

☐ All other countries add $12.00

TOTAL ENCLOSED _____

Please indicate method of payment:

☐ Check or money order, payable to American Wine Society

☐ Visa   ☐ Master Card   Expires _____

Account No.   Cardholder's signature

Index

Index

V. riparia *60, 61, 63, 66, 67*

V. rotundifolia *5, 60*

V. rupestris *60, 61, 63, 64, 65, 66, 67*

V. solonis *60*

V. Vinifera *4, 6, 10, 17, 22, 53, 59, 63, 66, 67*

V. vulpina *60*

varieties *4, 59*

Verdelet *39*

Vidal blanc *41, 65*

Vignoles *7*

Villard blanc *39, 41*

W

wax *43*

weeds *16, 17, 18, 47*

Wineries Unlimited *5*

winter *6, 8, 17, 21, 26, 46, 84, 86*

wire *15, 26, 35*